YUGOSLAVIA

The Theory and Practice of
Development Planning

YUGOSLAVIA

The Theory and Practice
of Development Planning

GEORGE MACESICH

Professor of Economics
The Florida State University

THE UNIVERSITY PRESS OF VIRGINIA

Charlottesville

THE UNIVERSITY PRESS OF VIRGINIA

© *1964 by the Rector and Visitors*
of the University of Virginia

FIRST PUBLISHED 1964

Library of Congress Catalog Card Number: 64–22631
Printed in the United States of America

In Memory of My Mother
MILKA TEPAVAC MACESICH

PREFACE

YUGOSLAVIA is a country undergoing continuous change in its institutions and economy if not in its political leadership. The country entered the postwar period with a strongly centralized government and economic system. Centralized planning coupled with a rigorous central government was the rule until the period following Yugoslavia's expulsion from the Cominform in 1948. Thereafter rapid changes occurred in the country. Decentralization of the government and economic activities was pursued with a vigor matched only by the previous drive toward centralization. Indeed, there is evidence that such decentralization has its local nationalistic overtones and may have gone too far, as illustrated by the unnecessary duplication of various productive facilities in the several republics. This "to and fro" movement in Yugoslavia was accomplished under essentially the same leadership that prevailed prior to the country's expulsion from the Cominform. The Yugoslav leadership embarked on an "independent road to socialism." Such an independent course of action reestablished the centuries-old Yugoslav "bridge" between East and West.

The planks of the bridge, whether of domestic origin or grown in the East or the West, have been hewn by the old independent Yugoslav mountaineers and paid for in "blood, sweat, and tears." The bridge has never remained closed for very long, nor has the traffic been exclusively one way. Failure to grasp the significance of the economic, cultural, and political bridge is to misunderstand current-day Yugoslavia and its tremendous, albeit hidden, influence on newly independent nations and on "Eastern countries," including the Soviet Union itself.

Some argue that the Soviet model consists of a strategy of development and a planning procedure. If this is correct, then Yugoslavia's "separate road to socialism" involves dropping the planning procedure of the Soviet model but keeping, for all practical purposes, that model's strategy of development. Since the country has also adopted in place of the Soviet's planning procedures many features usually associated with Western free-market economies, Yugoslavia's "separate road" is but a form of its centuries-old East-West bridge.

This book attempts to present a detailed analysis of the contemporary Yugoslav economy in the hope of providing additional insights into the processes of economic development and planning. In some respects this study supplements and updates, while at the same time drawing on, the work of such writers as Nikola Čobeljić, Bora Jelić, Branko Horvat, Branko Kubović, and Vidosav Tričković in Yugoslavia, Benjamin Ward, Albert Waterston, and Egon Neuberger in the United States, as well as others in Europe whose interest in the economy of Yugoslavia is well known.

Familiarity with the language, people, and country coupled with on-the-scene observation of Yugoslavia's economy in 1958, 1961, and 1963 has prompted me to undertake this study. I am indebted to many Yugoslavs who have given freely of their time. Their discussions, suggestions, and criticism were always constructive. Especially helpful have been the personnel of the National Bank (*Nardona Banka*), particularly Mr. Dimitrije Dimitrijević and Mr. Branko Mijović. Professors Ljubiša S. Adamović and Miloš Vučković, both of Belgrade University, Mr. Stojan Bulat, and Mr. Petar Madžarac have also contributed criticism and suggestions. Their aid has been indispensable to the completion of the study. Some have not always agreed, and some still do not, with the analysis and conclusions presented. My hope is that I have achieved scholarly objectivity; for that I alone am responsible.

Finally, I am indebted to my colleagues, Professors Žarko G.

Bilbija, Marshall R. Colberg, and Stephen J. Knezevich, to my brother, Mr. Walter Macesich, Jr., and to Professor Fritz Machlup for their patient reading of the manuscript and their many valuable comments and suggestions. I should also like to express my appreciation to Mrs. Gennelle Perry Jordan, Miss Rosalie Licata, and Mrs. Eddine Rivers Kessler for typing and proofreading the manuscript. My thanks are due also to the Graduate Research Council of Florida State University for financial assistance which helped make this study possible.

GEORGE MACESICH

Tallahassee, Florida
March 1964

CONTENTS

FIGURES

TABLES

YUGOSLAVIA

The Theory and Practice of
Development Planning

1.

THE POLITICAL AND SOCIAL ORGANIZATION

BACKGROUND

Many changes have occurred in Yugoslavia's political and social organization since 1950. These changes reflect the development of the country's "separate path to socialism" or what has come to be called "Titoism." This separate path is constructed by means of "decentralization and popular participation" at all levels in the affairs of the country. It is only by such means, argue the Yugoslavs, that a country can develop "true socialist democracy"—and principally because these means promote the "withering away of the state." It is not the purpose of this study to go into all the political and social ramifications in the development of Titoism in Yugoslavia. This chapter has the more modest aim of sketching only the salient features of the political and social organization in order that a clear understanding may be had of the operation of the economy.[1]

GOVERNMENT ON THE FEDERAL, REPUBLIC, AND LOCAL LEVELS

With the abandonment of the rigid Soviet type of sociopolitical organization the Yugoslavs have drawn liberally from human

[1] For a more detailed discussion, the reader is referred to Alex N. Dragnich, *Tito's Promised Land—Yugoslavia* (New Brunswick: Rutgers University Press, 1954) ; Fred

experience in reorganizing their institutional framework. George W. Hoffman and Fred Warner Neal aptly summarize these developments when they write that "the Yugoslavs dipped into not only the experience of the French Revolution and the early days of the Bolshevik Revolution but also American theory and practice. They came up with a system that as a whole was new and original, including certain institutions held to be unique in the annals of political and economic organization." [2]

The country is a federated state consisting of six republics, Serbia, Croatia, Slovenia, Bosnia-Hercegovina, Montenegro, Macedonia, and two autonomous provinces, Vojvodina and Kosovo-Metohija, within the republic of Serbia. [3] A constitution provides for delegated and enumerated powers. A unique executive-legislative arrangement and direct worker representatives in legislative bodies are two of the chief characteristics of the country's governmental organization. Another is the wide autonomy granted local government with the basic unit or commune (opština) largely responsible for coordinating and supervising all economic activity and social services in its territory. Popular participation ranges from nomination of candidates by voters' meetings to management of public but nongovernmental undertakings by private citizens or groups.

The federal system, which incorporates a considerable amount of America experience, is ostensibly designed to satisfy the aspirations of the various nationality groups. According to official Yugoslav pronouncements, such a structure corresponds on the whole to the national structure of the country. Each Yugoslav national

---

Warner Neal, *Titoism in Action* (Berkeley: University of California Press, 1958); George W. Hoffman and Fred Warner Neal, *Yugoslavia and the New Communism* (New York: Twentieth Century Fund, 1962); the contributions by Anton Vratuša, Jovan Djordjević and Najdan Pašic, Kiro Gligorov, Branka Savić, and Milka Minić and Miloš Macura to "The Yugoslav Commune," *International Social Science Journal*, no. 3 (1961), pp. 379–447; Stoyan Pribechevich, *Yugoslavia's Way: The Program of the League of Communists of Yugoslavia* (New York: All Nations Press, 1958). The author is responsible for all translations from Serbo-Croat into English.

[2] Hoffman and Neal, *op. cit.*, p. 212.

[3] See *ibid.* for more details.

group has presumably acquired its own separate unit. The republic of Bosnia-Hercegovina is the only unit within the six constituent republics and two autonomous regions which is not based on nationality. And the reason for this exception, according to official explanations, is that neither the Serbs, Croats, nor Moslems who inhabit the territory had a clear "majority." It is interesting to note that according to the 1953 census the republic contained 44.4 per cent Serbs, 23 per cent Croats, and 31.3 per cent Moslems.

Undoubtedly a division of the country according to nationality groups has helped smooth some of the internal friction that has characterized the country in the past. Official claims that a solution to the "prewar nationality problem" has been found cannot be accepted without some reservation. If the criteria applied in the establishment of the republic of Bosnia-Hercegovina and the two autonomous provinces of Vojvodina and Kosovo-Metohija within Serbia were also applied to the republic of Croatia, for example, then two additional autonomous provinces or two more republics would be called for. Thus Lika, Bania, Kordun, and Slavonia, in effect the old Austrian Military Frontier now within the current republic of Croatia, would qualify as one unit and Dalmatia on the Adriatic coast as another.[4] In these areas the Serbs and Dalmatians respectively constitute a majority and here, during World War II, the Ustaša, a Croatian lunatic fringe, attempted to remove this majority by wholesale massacres and forced conversion to Roman Catholicism. These measures were not successful. The current emphasis on communes or local areas should at least restore some semblance of autonomy to these Serbs and Dalmatians—a trend which began with the Constitution of 1953 and which is continued in the draft of the New Constitution of 1962, which was adopted in

[4] In addition to Gunther Erich Rothenberg, *The Austrian Military Border in Croatia, 1522-1747* (Urbana: The University of Illinois Press, 1960), an excellent though often overlooked study by Professor Lazo M. Kostich, *Sporni predeli Srba i Hrvata* ("Controversial Regions between Serbs and Croats") (Chicago: The American Institute for Balkan Affairs, 1957), is useful in giving insights into the problems of the Serbian majority in the areas within the present republic of Croatia. See also George Macesich, "Yugoslav Panorama," *Social Research*, Winter 1963, pp. 527–36.

1963.[5] Whether or not this is finally a recognition of an oversight on the part of the authorities it is difficult to say. It may be simply an attempt to realign communes in order to facilitate the handling of economic and administrative affairs. Thus far, in any case, the nationality problem manifests itself in forms that result in duplication of facilities, which results in considerable economic waste.

An important feature of the new constitution adopted in 1963 is the provision for a Constitutional Court. Patterned after the American Supreme Court and molded in its inception and organization in 1959 by advice from justices of the U. S. Supreme Court, the new Constitutional Court is to be given authority to pass on the constitutionality of the laws of both the Federal Assembly and the parliaments of the several republics as well as on constitutional questions raised with respect to government administration. It is to replace the Constitutional Commission of the Federal Assembly. The new court is to have both original and appellate jurisdiction and can act either on the basis of actual cases or on requests of social organizations and accused persons claiming violation of constitutional rights. Unlike the organization of the American Supreme Court, however, each of the ten members of the court is elected by the Federal Assembly for a ten-year term.

It would, of course, be erroneous to conclude that the principles underlying either the country's 1953 or its 1963 constitution are similar to those prevailing in the West or in the East, though they come much closer to the latter than to the former. Indeed, the new constitution provides for the Communist party as the "fundamental initiator of political activity." Unlike most constitutions in the West, Yugoslavia's constitution has much to say on the economic relations of individuals and society. In discussing the proposed new constitution in 1962, Vice-President Edward Kardelj, one of the country's leading political theorists, argued that

if the essence of the bourgeois-democratic system lies in the principle of ensuring the freest possible manipulation of capital by private owners,

[5] Union of Jurists' Association of Yugoslavia, *The Constitution of the Federal Socialist Republic of Yugoslavia: A Preliminary Draft* (Belgrade: Servis saveza udruženje pravnika Jugoslavije, 1962) .

the aim of our Constitutional order is to make it possible for producers to join production as freely as possible according to their abilities and inclinations, thus acquiring the right to manage the socially owned means of production and the right to take part in the distribution of income according to work performed in accordance with uniform social standards of evaluating the work of individuals. There is no other way to ensure socialist distribution of the social product and there can be no other criteria for this distribution. Any deviation from the above-mentioned principles would hamper socialist, economic, and social relations.[6]

It was the 1953 constitution which provided for the novel system of worker representation in the Council of Producers, which together with the Federal Council (as distinct from the Federal Executive Council) makes up the bicameral Federal Assembly or *Skupština*. The Federal Assembly represents national sovereignty and supreme government in the Yugoslav Federation.[7] It exercises the rights granted the Federation by the constitution either directly or through the President of the Republic and the Federal Council as its executives.

The Assembly has exclusive jurisdiction over such matters as constitutional amendments, general referendums, enactment of the Federal Economic Plan and Budget, enactment of basic decisions on foreign and domestic policy, declarations of a state of war, and the conclusion of peace. It elects and removes the President of the Republic, members of the Federal Executive Council, and federal judges. Its primary purpose, however, is to enact federal legislation. This is particularly important because the Federal Executive Council is not empowered to enact decrees with legal force except during times of mobilization and war.

There are two categories of deputies in the Federal Council: those directly elected by general, equal, and direct suffrage at the rate of one deputy per 60,000 inhabitants and those delegated by the assemblies of the several republics and the two autonomous provinces. The delegated deputies form a third council, the Coun-

---

[6] As reported in "Information Service Yugoslavia" Bulletin no. RN 323/62-E.

[7] For a more detailed analysis, see Aleksandar Jovanović, *Yugoslavia's State and Social System* (Belgrade: Jugoslavija Publishing House, 1960).

cil of Nationalities, which convenes only on special occasions to consider such questions as constitutional amendments, the draft of the Federal Economic Plan, and in general the relations between the several republics.

According to the 1953 constitution, the deputies in the Council of Producers were elected indirectly and separately, through special electoral bodies, by the industrial and agricultural producers. The number of deputies in each of the categories was determined by the proportion of the contributions of the category, i.e., industry or agriculture, to the country's gross national product as determined by the current Federal Economic Plan. Election of the deputies within each production category was on the basis of one deputy per 70,000 direct producers, the members of the producers' families being counted.

The 1963 constitution, however, eliminates the relationship between production and election and calls for the election of deputies to be based on population. In addition, the new constitution calls for the formation of additional producers' councils to encompass workers in the health service, social institutions, education, and culture.[8] Another major change is the appointment of a premier to serve under the president. The premier will relieve the president of much of the routine work, but the president will retain firm control.

The Federal Council and the Council of Producers are equals and possess three constitutional jurisdictions: equal, exclusive, and joint. In matters of equal jurisdiction relating to the economy, incomes, and social welfare the two bodies are equal. Should disagreement arise, the issue is considered by joint commissions of the two bodies. In the event no agreement is forthcoming, then the Assembly is dissolved and new elections are called.

The President of the Republic serves as chief of state, president of the Federal Council, and commander-in-chief of the armed forces. In effect, the president under the 1953 constitution was an executive of the Federal Assembly. He was elected from the mem-

[8] "Information Service Yugoslavia" Bulletin no. RN 323/62–E.

bers of the Assembly for the same four-year term as its members at a joint session of the two bodies. The candidate receiving an absolute majority of the Assembly was deemed elected. This has been changed under the 1963 constitution to grant Tito life tenure and his successors two consecutive terms of four years each.

Sharing the executive powers of the Assembly with the president is the Federal Executive Council. The Council is responsible for all political executive affairs under federal jurisdiction. It does not possess complete executive powers but exercises only those related to the political side of such functions. Unlike the situation as it existed under the 1946 Stalinist type of constitution, however, the Constitution of 1953 provides that the Federal Council discharge only such political functions as are explicitly allocated to it by law. On this score there appears to be little change in the 1963 constitution.

The Federal Assembly elects and dismisses members of the Executive Council. Members of the Council are elected at the first joint session of the Assembly. It remains in power, however, even after the Assembly is dissolved and until new elections occur. It sets the dates of elections.

Although the members of the Federal Executive Council are not the heads of the federal bodies of the federal administration, the Secretaries of State for Foreign Affairs and National Defenses must be members of the Council. The Council itself sets the directives for and supervises the work of the federal administration. The various bodies of the federal administration are required to submit regular reports to the Council, which serve as the basis for the Council's recommendation to the various administrative bodies. The Council also concerns itself with the work of the public prosecutor and the public attorney's office, both of which it appoints and dismisses.

The Federal Executive Council is not considered superior to the several councils of the republics. It does, however, have the right to pass on the legality of the work of the republic councils. Thus it may stay a decree and other acts of the republic councils that it considers at odds with federal acts or decrees. The Supreme Court under the 1963 constitution may relieve the Executive Council of this power.

Under the law the various units of the federal administration are responsible for enforcing the law, implementing economic plans, and performing various duties for the representative bodies and their executives. The administration is organized on federal and communal systems, which is to say that there are separate federal, republic, district, and communal bodies. Although there is a horizontal separation of the bodies at these various levels, they operate as a unitary system and their relations are prescribed by law according to specific rights and duties.

Organization on republic levels differs only slightly from that on the federal level. The republics do not have councils of nationalities in their assemblies nor presidents of the republic. The president of the executive council of a republic may veto anything passed by the council with which he is in disagreement. These councils are the principal organs for administration, with powers similar to those of the federal secretariats.

The organization of government in the autonomous province of Vojvodina does not differ significantly from that of the republics. The province has an assembly consisting of two councils, an executive council, a president of the executive council, and various administrative bodies similar to those of the republican bodies.

In the autonomous province of Kosovo-Metohija the government is organized partly along the lines of the republics and partly on the principle of organization of the people's committee, which is to say that the province has no representative assembly. The Regional People's Committee in the province does, however, have an executive council as its executive political body. The administrative bodies are the same as those found in the province of Vojvodina except that there is no Secretariat for Judicial Affairs.

Similar to the Federation and the republics, the district as a political unit has rights and duties prescribed by law and contained in the district's statute. The district's people's committee is the supreme body of government in the district. The rights and duties of the district, however, are not exercised only through the committee. Many, for example, are exercised through the meetings of the electorate.

The commune or municipality as legally defined is the "basic political territorial organization of self-government of the working people and the fundamental social and economic community of the inhabitants of the municipal territory." It exercises all the rights and duties of government except those specifically delegated to district, republic, or Federation. In the exercise of "social affairs" legal presumption is in favor of the municipality.

LEAGUE OF COMMUNISTS AND THE SOCIALIST ALLIANCE

No account of the country's government is complete without a word about the Communist party, or the League of Communists as it is now called.[9] According to official pronouncements, party members have not received preferential treatment since 1950. With the coming of decentralization the highly centralized party apparatus was out of step with developments. In 1952 at the Fourth Plenum of the Central Committee of the Yugoslav party a series of directives was issued applying the principles of decentralization to the party and limiting its direct role in local government and economic matters. And in November of that year the Sixth Party Congress considerably altered the party's methods of operation.

Henceforth the party was to confine itself to "political and ideological education." Party units were not to impose their will "directly" nor were party members to use their positions to give orders. Members were to exert their influence as individuals and as members of the various governing bodies. According to Vice-President Kardelj, this meant an end to the party's monopoly. To the more skeptical, however, it simply meant that the party would exercise control in more sophisticated ways.

It is the Socialist Alliance of Working People of Yugoslavia,

[9] See the references cited in note 1, especially Pribechevich's *Yugoslavia's Way.*

before 1953 known as the People's Front, that the Yugoslavs consider important in dealing with concrete political and social questions. Since 1961 the Socialist Alliance has no longer included everyone and every type of organization in the country as it once did. It now includes the League of Communists and some of the unions and youth organizations.

2.

THE COMMUNE

THE CONCEPT OF LOCAL SELF-GOVERNMENT

The commune is the basic territorial unit in Yugoslavia. Continual consolidation since the mid-1950's has reduced the number and increased the size of these local units until by 1960 there were 800 communes with an average population of 22,500 per unit; these are grouped into 75 districts with an average population of 250,000 per district.

The concept of local government expressed in these communes differs considerably from that of Western countries. According to Professors Jovan Djordjević and Najdan Pašić "local self-government in Yugoslavia is an institution of the Federal Constitution in which it finds both its authority and its guarantee. Contrary to the Anglo-American theory that local self-government is an expression and a creation of Parliament (England) or of the Federated States (in the United States), political and constitutional practice in Yugoslavia treats local self-government as an expression of the citizens' fundamental political right to govern themselves." Elsewhere in their study they write that it is only in those countries which have provided for a large measure of local self-government (the United States, United Kingdom, Switzerland, and Sweden) that parliamentary institutions have thrived and lasted. [1]

[1] Jovan Djordjević and Najdan Pašić, "The Communal Self-Government System in Yugoslavia," *International Social Science Journal*, no. 3 (1961), p. 389.

The Yugoslav commune apparently is something more than a simple device for local self-government. It is the "fundamental cell of future socialist society; more precisely, it now represents a socio-economic community within which new socialist social relationships are being established on the basis of social ownership of means of production and, in rural areas, on different forms of socialization or co-operation and limitation of individual ownership of land among peasants." [2] Indeed, the over-all picture suggests that the commune is a "structure removed from State control [and] made up of autonomous economic organizations within a commune (enterprises, co-operatives, etc.) and those autonomous institutions providing social services (schools, cultural and artistic institutions, hospitals and health establishments, social and community institutions, etc.)." [3] For all practical purposes it would seem that "the communal system is a sort of symbiosis of local self-government and the mechanism of social self-administration in the local communities. To emphasize this wider significance of local self-government, it would be better to use the terms 'communal system' or 'communal sociopolitical organization.'" [4] In Appendix 1 there are presented extracts from the statutes of the commune of Kranj in the republic of Slovenia. A close scrutiny of these statutes and the table of organization reveals that at least on paper the commune is indeed a potent force for promoting local self-government.

The scope of the commune's varying activities has been summarized as follows:

Functional means. The commune is completely autonomous as regards the establishment of its economic plan and budget and the setting up of enterprises and communal institutions—cultural, educational, health and social.

Legislative and legal means. The commune and district adopt their own regulatory provisions . . . which may include administrative penalties.

[2] *Ibid.,* p. 390.
[3] *Ibid.,* p. 391.
[4] *Ibid.*

Administrative means. The commune applies directly the laws, rules and regulations laid down by higher authorities; it is also responsible for administrative proceedings and administrative-penal proceedings of first instance, and other administrative functions in all matters, except where the application of laws, rules and regulations has been entrusted to other lower organs. . . .

Means for self-organization and protection of self-government. The commune decides on the organization and operation of its organs and institutions, appoints its employees and initiates proceedings for appeal for the protection of the rights of self-government in cases where a rule or regulation or any other act of the higher organs of the State violates one of its legal rights.

Means for the protection of general legality. The commune may repeal or declare null and void the unlawful acts of an economic organization (enterprise) or autonomous institution (school, hospital, artistic and cultural institutions, etc.) .[5]

ECONOMIC SIGNIFICANCE OF COMMUNES

Although the political and social aspects of communes are important in themselves, it is only their economic aspects that will be considered in this study. Over-all planning of the pre-1952 type has been unable to come to grips with problems resulting from the geographically uneven economic development that has taken place in the country over the centuries. Many of these problems appear more tractable at the level of the commune, where at least local initiative, interest, and knowledge can be combined with various forms of help from republic and federal sources. In some respects it is an arrangement which even the United States Chamber of Commerce would approve. Local initiative rather than republic or federal impulsion provides the motivating force for economic development.

Without access to necessary economic resources, such initiative would be nothing more than wishful thinking. In Yugoslavia the commune as well as the district obtains funds in several ways. Certain sources of revenue for the communes and districts are

[5] *Ibid.,* p. 398.

established by federal law. Moreover, each commune and district is guaranteed by law the ownership of its own resources. Each commune, moreover, is entitled to a minimum of 29 per cent of the total revenue of its territory.

A commune's regular revenue comes from various taxes. Taxes on workers' personal incomes and the incomes of economic enterprises are important sources of revenue, although the federal authorities and the Federal Plan establish these taxes. At the disposal of the commune are also land taxes, inheritance taxes, taxes on gifts, special wage taxes paid by economic enterprises, and turnover taxes. Some of these revenues are channeled into autonomous or extrabudgetary funds established for the purpose of financing investment in the commune or district. Investment funds for road building and maintenance, on both district and commune levels, and funds for housing construction are examples. Table 1 gives an idea of the resources at the disposal of communes.

TABLE 1. Distribution of budgetary and planning resources among the principal beneficiaries in 1959

	Resources	
	IN BILLIONS OF DINARS	PER CENT
Federal level	628.1	38.3
Republics	277.7	16.9
Communes	450.7	27.6
Economic organization	282.7	17.2
Total	1,639.2	100

Source: Kiro Gligorov, "The Communal Economy," *International Social Science Journal*, no. 3 (1961), p. 409.

It shows that the communes and economic organization have at their disposal almost 45 per cent of the resources allocated for various budgetary and planning purposes. The importance of the communes and economic organizations in providing funds for economic development is underscored by the fact that the bulk of the federal level's share is allocated for defense, export promotion, external debt payment, and servicing.

The commune plays one of its principal roles in economic planning. Here its role appears to be one of integrating, in a sense, the various plans of economic enterprise within its territory. The commune, for example, organizes a systematic survey of the various factors that affect the economic development of its area, thereby providing economic intelligence in the form of data and analyses. This is particularly important in view of the fact that such data and analyses take into consideration the recommendations and aspirations of the republic and federal levels of government. One should not conclude that the communes are little more than messenger boys for the upper levels of government. In fact, the communes provide the various levels of government with some idea of what is, in their view, realistically possible in their areas, though, paradoxically, such views sometimes tend to be idealistic.

In the distribution of the investment resources at its disposal a commune has an important effect on the economic development of its territory. By making its projects attractive, the commune not only may obtain the cooperation of economic enterprises within its territory but it may attract funds from the republic or the Federation. And, indeed, joint ventures of two or more communes on projects that are favorably looked upon by a republic or the Federation are a sure way of supplementing a commune's investment resources. In effect, a commune must keep one eye on the desires and wishes of the upper levels of government if it is to carry out projects that are beyond its means.

A commune must underwrite the establishment of new firms in its territory. In cases of failure the commune shares a good deal of the financial responsibility involved. To be sure, some of the responsibility is lifted from the commune when once a firm's worker-managers take over the management. As for the expansion of existing firms, this also is the responsibility of a firm's worker-managers.

3.

A SURVEY OF THE ECONOMY

NATIONAL INCOME AND POPULATION

To judge from available evidence the performance of the Yugoslavian economy in the period from 1947 to 1960 has gone from bad to better. In the period from 1947 to 1952, when the economy was in a strait jacket of the Soviet type, national income (in 1956 prices) grew at approximately an average annual rate of 1 per cent, and the social product, which is the sum of national income and a depreciation component and similar to gross national product, at approximately an average annual rate of 2.2 per cent.[1] By contrast, in a comparable period following World War I, 1923–29, when a relatively free economic system was in operation, national income (in 1938 prices) grew at an average rate of 3.5 per cent. Indeed, even during the difficult period of 1930–39 national income grew at an average annual rate of 2.4 per cent.[2] When such evidence is coupled with the post-1948 political situation, it is little wonder that the Yugoslavs dropped the planning apparatus of the Soviet model and adopted a more pragmatic economic policy.

Once the Soviet model's planning apparatus was dropped and

[1] *Statistički godišnjak FNRJ* 1961 ("Statistical Yearbook FNRJ 1961"; Belgrade: Savezni zavod za statistiku ["Federal Institute of Statistics"]), pp. 98–99. Published yearly, hereafter only title and year will be given.

[2] Steven Stajić, "Realni nacionalni dohodak Jugoslavije" ("Real National Income of Yugoslavia"), a paper presented in Belgrade before the Conference of the Yugoslav Statistical Association, June 18–20, 1959.

16

the "Yugoslav experiment" of "decentralization" became a reality, the performance of the economy improved remarkably. In the period from 1952 to 1960 national income increased at an average annual rate of approximately 10.6 per cent and the social product at an average annual rate of approximately 10 per cent.[3] These results tend to confirm to the Yugoslavs as well as others the "correctness" of their approach and the viability of their economy. On the other hand, since 1952 the economy has been increasingly feeling the effects of open inflation, with the stock of money almost doubling and the general level of prices increasing by almost 60 per cent in the period from 1952 to 1960. More will be said about the stock of money and prices in a latter chapter. At this point it is sufficient to note that it is more accurate to judge the performance of the economy in terms of 1952 than 1960 prices. Unfortunately, comparable data for the entire period are not available.

Economic, statistical, and other factors blur the significance of the economy's performance. Thus the economic blockade against Yugoslavia instituted in 1948 by the Soviet East shut off the flow of critical materials to the economy. Economic independence and military defense were stressed with the result that resources needed elsewhere were diverted to these objectives. Economic factors gave way to strictly military considerations in the allocation of funds. Investment in agriculture, social services, and the production of consumer goods declined during 1948–52. One economist estimates that the economic blockade cost the Yugoslav economy a probable drop of about 30 per cent in its development rate—which presumably means in the growth of national income.[4] Moreover, two severe droughts, in 1950 and 1952, decreased agricultural production, which at the time was an especially important factor in the composition of national output and income. To this is usually added the severity of destruction that occurred in Yugoslavia during World War II. This destruction should not be minimized, but it should be noted that Serbia was,

[3] *Statistički godišnjak 1961*, pp. 98–99.
[4] Branko Horvat, "The Characteristics of Yugoslav Economic Development," *Socialist Thought and Practice*, no. 1, p. 4.

for all practical purposes, in constant warfare from 1912 to 1918 (in two Balkan Wars and World War I). Damages to life and property were as extensive then if indeed not greater than those that occurred in the country during World War II. Yet Serbia recovered quite rapidly following World War I, as did the rest of the Yugoslav territories.

According to the Federal Statistical Institute, which is responsible for the compilation of the *Statistical Year Book* ("Statistički Godišnjak"), data incorporated in national income and social product accounts for the socialist sector are based on the settlement accounts of economic organizations. All of the economic organizations in the socialist sector of the economy have been included except those that failed during the financial year. One consequence of such a procedure may be that total national income for the period is underestimated.

The method of classification of economic enterprises, on the other hand, may lead to double counting and so overstate national income. As indicated by the Federal Statistical Institute, an economic enterprise has been taken as the basic unit of observation in computation of the national income. It is classified according to its predominant activity. Difficulties may arise, however, when enterprises with auxiliary activities are considered. For example, a considerable part of the forestry activity may spill over and be counted again under woodworking. Similarly, income derived from industrial power plants may erroneously be included in the electrical energy sector as well. Care has been taken by the institute, however, to avoid such spill-overs as far as possible so that the national income estimates are not greatly unbalanced as a consequence.

Much more important as possible sources of error in national income are the estimates for income in the private sector of the economy. The private sector includes the bulk of agriculture, arts and crafts, and important segments of construction, transport, and board and lodging services. The income of the private sector of agriculture has been estimated on the basis of agricultural statistics relating to the production of plants and the number of livestock, as well as on the basis of price statistics. The figures also include estimates of income derived by private farmers in forestry and auxiliary agricultural activities. The direction of bias in such estimates is, for all practical purposes, unknown. In Yugoslavia private farmers may sell their produce at free market prices. These prices are usually above the average prices used in computing official income estimates, with the result that the estimates are biased downward. On the other hand, if price data for the better quality output of the larger farms are employed in computing the income of the poorer farms that dominate the private agricultural scene, the results may very well overestimate the income derived from the private sector of agriculture.

Similarly, the income of the private sector of arts and crafts may be biased in an unknown direction, though most probably downward. The income in this sector is estimated on the basis of the number of craftsmen, the amount of income in the cooperative sector of arts and crafts, and other unspecified data (but presumably tax returns). Insofar as private craftsmen receive the bulk of their pay in cash, together with the fact that the socialist counterpart is one of the most underdeveloped sectors of the economy, private craftsmen may well have a larger income than official figures indicate. If we take newspaper reports seriously, this has indeed been the case in the past few years.

The method of computing national income results in a downward bias in the estimates. The method is based on the so-called "productive activities" such as manufacturing, agriculture, forestry, construction, "productive" arts and crafts, transport, trade, and board and lodging services. The national income figures do not include such "nonproductive" activities as work in personal services, the government, education, the liberal professions, and health and sanitation. The national income estimates are presented in Table 2.

Much of the effort in postwar Yugoslavia has gone into changing the relative positions of agriculture and industry (including mining). The effort has met with success in that the structure of the national income has been altered radically since 1939. To

TABLE 2. National income, 1947–61 *(in billions of dinars and in 1956 prices)*

	1947	1948	1949	1950	1951	1952	1953	1954	1955	1956	1957	1958	1959	1960	1961
Total economy	966	1183	1261	1131	1241	1051	1258	1243	1455	1444	1780	1811	2130	2249	2341
Industry	316	401	430	428	402	392	440	507	579	629	732	817	896	1026	1087
Agriculture	396	461	473	345	508	335	483	425	485	421	588	502	681	594	576
Forestry	38	50	61	50	43	37	28	28	29	29	31	28	34	39	41
Construction	61	80	92	85	63	59	69	73	71	65	78	83	92	102	111
Transport	41	54	66	71	68	60	66	71	84	86	99	109	121	143	150
Trade	73	95	94	100	101	107	110	117	131	135	161	192	198	225	242
Crafts	41	42	45	52	56	61	62	72	76	79	91	100	108	120	134

Source: *Statistički godišnjak FNRJ 1962* (Belgrade: Savezni zavod za statistiku, 1962), p. 98.

TABLE 3. National income by industry in 1939, 1960, and 1961
(*in percentages*)

Branch	1939	1960	1961
Total economy	100	100	100
Industry and mining	26.8	45.6	46.4
Agriculture	44.3	26.4	24.6
Forestry	4.6	1.2	1.8
Construction	2.5	1.5	4.7
Transport and communication	6.6	6.4	6.4
Trade, board and lodging services, and tourism	8.1	10.0	10.3
Crafts	7.1	5.4	5.8

Source: Research Department, National Bank of Yugoslavia.

judge from data contained in Table 3, industry and mining in
1960 accounted for over 46 per cent of the national income
compared to less than 27 per cent in 1939. Agriculture's share, on
the other hand, declined from over 44 per cent in 1939 to under 25
per cent in 1960.

Yugoslavia's population (Table 4) has for the most part re-

TABLE 4. Population, 1939 and 1947–62 (*in thousands*)

Year	Population	Year	Population
1939	15,596	1955	17,519
1947	15,679	1956	17,685
1948	15,901	1957	17,859
1949	16,133	1958	18,018
1950	16,346	1959	18,214
1951	16,588	1960	18,402
1952	16,798	1961	18,607
1953	17,048	1962	18,837
1954	17,284		

Source: *Statistički godišnjak FNRJ 1961* and *SFRJ 1963* (Belgrade: Savezni zavod za statistiku, 1961 and
1963), pp. 52 (*1961*), 81 (*1963*).

covered from the severe blow suffered during World War II when approximately 1,700,000 persons were lost. The war loss and subsequent losses through emigration have come primarily from the 25–45-age group. Needless to say, losses from this group have had particularly harsh effects on the economy in general. It will be some time before the country recovers from these effects.

EMPLOYMENT, PERSONAL INCOME,
AND LIVING STANDARDS

The relative decline in agriculture suggested by the changed structure of national income is also evidenced by the distribution of the labor force according to origin of income. In 1939 approximately 75 per cent of the Yugoslav people derived their income from agriculture; by 1948 the figure dropped to 68.3 per cent. In 1953, when the new economic system was in operation, the figure

TABLE 5. Employment, September 1956–62 (*in thousands*)

Sector	1956	1957	1958	1959	1960	1961	1962
Total	2,320	2,478	2,649	2,827	3,070	3,372	3,443
Industry and mining	861	924	995	1,048	1,134	1,147	1,184
Agriculture	199	198	235	264	281	360	356
Forestry	30	33	37	38	48	82	93
Construction	234	240	284	294	330	373	350
Transport	182	188	161	177	187	206	231
Trade and board and lodging services	208	218	222	237	260	315	328
Arts and crafts	167	194	202	216	244	265	255
Public utilities	43	51	59	67	75	85	97
Culture and education	137	150	164	174	183	194	209
Social welfare	100	108	116	124	136	154	159
Government *	118	126	124	132	133	126	112
Other †	41	48	50	56	59	65	69

Source: *Statistički godišnjak 1963*, p. 99.
* Includes judicature.
† Includes finance and credit associations, economic associations, occupational associations, and political and social organizations.

dropped to 60.9 per cent, and in 1960 it declined to about 50 per cent.[5]

Industry and mining were the chief beneficiaries of this transfer of workers from agriculture. Table 5 summarizes employment by sectors of the economy. It suggests that industry and mining are the principal employment outlets in the economy, although employment increased in all sectors in the period from 1956 to 1960.

The data on employment presented in Table 5 are, however, incomplete. They do not include persons employed in the institutions and public offices of the State Secretariat for People's Defense, the State Secretariat for Home Affairs and the economic organizations under its jurisdiction, and the staff of all government branches on duty abroad. These numbers, however, do not appear to be significant.

Unemployment as registered by people seeking employment through the labor exchanges from 1955 to 1962 was as follows:

1955	67,233	1959	161,633
1956	99,338	1960	159,230
1957	115,904	1961	191,283
1958	132,004	1962	236,667

These figures indicate that persons seeking employment rose rapidly from 1955 through 1959 and then dropped slightly in 1960. Most of the 159,230 people registered in 1960, for example, were unskilled workers and presumably recent migrants from agriculture. The figures suggest the continuing decline in agricultural pursuits as well as the problems that such rapid displacements create.

The personal income data presented in Table 6 are based on surveys covering (1) 277 selected enterprises engaged in manufacturing, mining, and quarrying that employ about 33 per cent of the labor force engaged in industry; (2) 105 agricultural enterprises that employ about 15 per cent of those engaged in agriculture; (3) 39 building enterprises with about 26 per cent of the

[5] Information supplied by the Research Department, National Bank of Yugoslavia.

TABLE 6. Nominal and real personal income of "workers and employees," 1956–61 (monthly averages in dinars; 1960 = 100 for real income)

	"WORKERS"			"EMPLOYEES"		
	Total		Nominal	Total		Nominal
Year	NOMINAL	REAL	Regular	NOMINAL	REAL	Regular
1956	9,780	71	9,230	12,770	66	11,730
1957	11,620	83	10,340	16,320	81	13,750
1958	12,270	81	10,960	16,870	83	14,890
1959	13,800	91	12,500	19,620	94	17,220
1960	16,300	100	14,820	23,240	100	20,560
1961	18,860	105	17,190	27,850	110	24,690

Source: *Statistički godišnjak 1962*, p. 251.

persons employed in this sector; (4) 813 trade and board and lodging service establishments employing 31 per cent of people engaged in this activity. The enterprises selected are those considered to be most important in their particular sectors of the economy.

The data are based on monthly reports of the receipts of employed persons paid according to the work performed and on regulations regarding personal earnings in force during the period under review. Total personal receipts include also overtime payments, awards, and profit shares above earnings fixed by earning rules. For 1960 total personal income data include contributions paid from earnings into special budgets and social insurance funds so that in effect these data are for gross earnings. In order to make the 1960 data comparable with those of earlier years the Federal Statistical Institute applied various coefficients to the 1960 data to convert them into net receipts. These estimates understate personal incomes because they do not include certain benefits such as receipts in kind, transportation, children's allowances, compensation for separated family life, and certain other receipts realized under special rules and regulations.

The classifications "workers" and "employees" deserve some comment in view of their peculiar connotation in Yugoslavia. The category "worker" applies to those engaged primarily in manual work in manufacturing processes, trade, and transportation. "Employees" on the other hand are those engaged in what are considered intellectual activities. For example, managers, technicians, and clerical workers are included in the "employee" category because they participate intellectually rather than physically in economic activity.

The data in Table 6 show the relatively higher incomes of the skilled individuals in the economy and, by implication, the shortage of such individuals.

If the official rate of exchange prevailing in 1961—750 dinars to a dollar—is applied, monthly incomes are indeed modest. The average monthly income of a skilled worker in 1960 amounted to a little less than $31. Such comparisons are not, however, particularly meaningful owing to differences in the purchasing power of the two currencies, i.e., $31 will go much farther in Yugoslavia than in the United States. There are, however, significant differences among the several republics in the monthly incomes of both the unskilled and skilled members of the labor force. The highest average monthly incomes reported in 1960 obtained in Slovenia, which had an average of 19,600 dinars for unskilled workers and 29,130 dinars for skilled workers. In the largest and most important republic, Serbia, unskilled workers received a monthly average of 15,340 dinars while skilled workers averaged 21,510 dinars. Wages in the remaining four republics, Bosnia-Hercegovina, Croatia, Macedonia, and Montenegro, were generally similar to those in Serbia. Croatia reported average monthly incomes slightly above Serbian: 16,950 dinars for unskilled workers and 24,410 dinars for skilled workers in 1960. The poorest of the republics, Macedonia, reported a monthly average income for unskilled workers of 12,530 dinars and 18,740 dinars for skilled workers. Montenegro, long considered one of the most backward economic areas of the country, has done relatively well with an average monthly income for unskilled workers of 13,930 dinars and 21,550 dinars for skilled workers. These differences in incomes are the source of much interrepublic friction and lead to a scramble for federal assistance and "pork barrel" legislation of the type so familiar in American politics. In Yugoslavia the problem is further complicated by various nationality aspirations.

Some idea of the standard of living in the country is available from surveys of farm families and of four-member families of unskilled and skilled workers. Table 7 shows the expenditures of farming households. A survey conducted in 1959 by the Federal Statistical Institute covered 2,666 households. The households included 35 households with one member; 242 with two; 341 with three; 428 with four; 463 with five; 438 with six; 289 with seven; 156 with nine and ten, 52 with eleven and twelve; and 22 with thirteen or more. The total income of these households was computed on the basis of consumption in kind, cash receipts from the sale of produce, and cash receipts from employment outside the farm. The value of consumption was computed on the basis of the sale prices of the products sold by the farm. The total income did not include such irregular receipts as loans, sales of immovables, and dowries. The data in Table 7 demonstrate clearly the differences between the several republics. Common to all of them is the fact that about 60 per cent of the expenditures per household member are for "food and beverage." Clothing is the next largest category, accounting for over 13 per cent of the total expenditures. What these figures suggest is that the typical Yugoslav farm family is far from affluent.

Urban dwellers, as indicated by surveys of unskilled and skilled workers' families with four members, are better off than dwellers in rural areas. In 1960 the Federal Statistical Institute conducted a survey of income and expenditures in 638 "workers' " and 561 "employees' " families in thirty-seven urban areas. Each family consisted of a husband, wife, and two children under eighteen years of age. The husband was the only employed member, and the family received children's allowances. The results of the survey are presented in Table 8.

The data are interesting in that they indicate that about 70 per

	Yugoslavia		Serbia		Croatia		Slovenia		Bosnia-Hercegovina		Macedonia		Montenegro	
	1960	1960	1959	1960	1959	1960	1959	1960	1959	1960	1959	1960	1959	1960
Total	50,273	55,074	45,140	50,491	62,533	70,226	71,978	78,295	39,939	47,714	43,478	46,015	45,710	53,377
Food & beverage	30,965	33,145	27,141	29,158	38,066	43,000	43,689	44,659	25,666	28,692	26,941	27,063	30,469	36,213
Tobacco	1,291	1,382	1,140	1,281	1,644	1,727	1,400	1,500	1,470	1,523	687	698	1,500	1,902
Clothing	7,200	7,982	6,807	7,947	9,289	9,886	9,867	11,136	5,455	6,000	6,119	7,778	5,677	6,426
Rent & utilities	4,436	7,873	4,456	5,000	4,822	5,568	7,022	7,955	3,303	3,492	3,761	3,794	3,290	3,623
Furnishings	2,436	3,109	1,982	2,860	2,978	3,523	4,156	6,136	1,742	1,938	2,791	2,952	1,806	1,328
Hygiene & health	1,109	1,273	1,000	1,175	1,578	1,886	1,822	2,068	697	877	985	1,016	548	721
Culture	836	1,146	877	1,052	978	1,318	1,400	1,682	318	723	687	1,016	837	1,475
Other	2,000	2,164	1,737	2,018	3,178	3,318	2,622	3,159	1,288	1,169	1,507	1,698	1,581	1,689

Source: Statistički godišnjak 1961 and 1962, pp. 443 (1961), 437 (1962).

TABLE 8. Average monthly income and expenditures of four-member "workers' " and "employees' " families in 1960 and 1961 (*in dinars*)

	"*Workers'* " Families		"*Employees'* " Families	
	1960	*1961*	*1960*	*1961*
I. Total available resources	33,336	38,270	42,557	49,799
Income	30,547	35,039	38,301	45,293
From regular employment	21,241	24,820	28,293	33,900
Regular wages	18,057	20,718	23,553	27,699
Profit	1,516	1,806	1,378	1,861
Bonuses	640	725	1,638	1,990
Overtime	1,028	1,571	1,724	2,350
Outside employment	611	787	863	758
Children's allowances	6,000	6,160	6,022	6,125
Rent receipts, sales, etc.	937	1,337	1,094	1,787
Gifts	585	595	627	994
Other	1,173	1,340	1,402	1,729
Credit, loans & savings	2,789	3,231	4,256	4,506
Consumer credit	1,334	1,850	1,908	2,334
II. Utilized resources	33,279	38,271	42,502	49,807
Expenditures	29,462	34,082	36,803	43,302
Living costs	28,625	33,147	35,950	42,251
Food	13,781	16,487	15,724	19,065
Tobacco & beverage	1,506	1,785	1,588	1,926
Clothing	4,651	4,788	6,243	6,635
Rent	1,321	1,838	1,950	2,480
Utilities	1,645	1,662	1,929	1,938
Furnishings	1,776	2,227	2,565	3,156
Hygiene	830	978	1,096	1,295
Culture	1,547	2,031	2,464	3,412
Other	1,568	1,351	2,391	2,344
Expenditures for holding and estate	688	778	582	801
Losses and gifts	149	157	271	250
Repayment of credit & savings	3,817	4,189	5,699	6,505
Consumer credit	2,214	2,444	2,828	3,519

Source: *Statistički godišnjak 1961* and *1962*, pp. 444–45 (*1961*), 438–39 (*1962*).

cent of "workers' " incomes come from regular employment and the remainder from various other categories, the two most important being children's allowances and profit shares. The same is true of the incomes of "employees." Urban families spend something over 40 per cent for food and beverages. This figure is considerably higher than that spent by urban families in some of the more economically advanced countries.

Table 8 suggests that urban dwellers spend only a little over 5 per cent of their available resources on housing. This is the result of rent controls; as a consequence of the low rents the problem of housing continues to be critical. The rapid inflow into the towns has intensified the problem. Two examples will suffice. In the towns of the province of Vojvodina, one of the richest areas, there are 70,000 single persons and over two-thirds of them are without adequate housing.[6] The province plans to rectify the situation with the construction of 48,000 new units for single persons within the next couple of years. But by the time that new housing is completed the continuing inflow from the countryside will require additional units. In Kraljevo, Serbia, 500 of the 1,200 people employed by the large Magnohrom works still live in their villages and commute because of the lack of housing.[7] The enterprise expects to solve this problem in the "near future" when additional housing units are completed.

The educational system also feels the stresses and strains of economic change. Rapid population shifts have placed a heavy burden on already overtaxed facilities. For example, in Nikšić, Montenegro, the site of an important industrial complex, schools are operating in three shifts and may even go to four, although 45 per cent of the community's budget goes for schools.[8] In the countryside around Nikšić children walk for hours to get to school. The situation is not much better in the other republics. Because of a scarcity of teachers vigorous bidding for their services is common. Montenegro, for example, has charged that 2,500 of its

[6] *Politika* (Belgrade), Nov. 22, 1961, p. 7.
[7] *Ibid.*, Nov. 15, 1961, p. 7.
[8] *Ibid.*, Nov. 22, 1961, p. 9.

educators and technicians have left for Bosnia in the past few years at the inducement of traveling Bosnian "salesmen" with "briefcases loaded with money."[9]

Although health facilities have lagged behind the rapid economic development of the country, important strides have been made in providing such facilities and raising the general level of health of the population. Between 1949 and 1958 more than 3,061 polyclinical outpatient and specialized surgeries were organized, and hospital beds were extended by some 34,000.[10] To itemize, the number of outpatient polyclinics rose from 1,144 to 2,734, dental offices from 441 to 1,214, antituberculosis clinics from 145 to 229, health facilities for women and children from 725 to 1,160, school clinics from 53 to 232, and the total number of hospital beds from 50,738 to 85,201.

To judge from population data, a steady fall in the death rate has occurred. In 1945 the rate stood at 14.9 per 1,000, in 1947 at 12.7, and in 1958 at 9.2. These rates are still high in comparison with those in more developed countries. Infectious, parasital, and other diseases characteristic of underdeveloped areas are tending to disappear in Yugoslavia. As causes of death they have been replaced by diseases common in industrially developed countries such as heart disease and cancer. The higher figures for the latter are probably also the consequence of better and more accurate diagnosis and reporting. Since private medical and dental practice has been curtailed, and indeed for all practical purposes eliminated, the situation of individuals who are not members of the national health insurance program is grim.

Improving the quality of the human agent has apparently received considerable attention. To their credit the Yugoslavs have realized the importance to their economy of improving the human agent even though they term such investment "noneconomic." Table 9 summarizes the progress made in providing the institutions which make such improvement possible.

Higher education received particular attention in the Recom-

[9] *Ibid.*, Nov. 11, 1961, p. 10.
[10] *Statistički kalendar 1961* (Belgrade: Federal Institute of Statistics, 1961).

TABLE 9. Enrollment and instructors in the academic years 1938/39, 1958/59, and 1961/62

Type of school	1938/39			1958/59			1961/62		
	No. of schools	Enrollment	Instructors	No. of schools	Enrollment	Instructors	No. of schools	Enrollment	Instructors
Primary schools *	9,190	1,470,973	34,663	14,342	2,426,920	79,686	14,568	2,895,694	89,611
Secondary schools *	205	125,098	5,607	254	77,574	4,894	275	94,651	5,512
Secondary teachers' college	37	4,268	555	77	23,648	1,698	108	30,335	2,005
Vocational schools	53	10,689	879	257	76,257	6,262	490	130,465	9,465
Art schools	5	603	136	40	3,822	1,100	47	4,408	1,213
Schools for skilled workmen	766	69,737	6,174	741	124,134	9,463	692	140,353	6,697
Other jr. vocational schools	4	135	23	49	3,102	678	43	3,110	572
Special schools	21	3,175	232	185	8,277	996	250	11,458	1,275
Adult education schools	0	0	0	722	47,958	5,946	1,007	73,040	6,119
School for complementary education	45	6,578	452	186	19,401	1,492	154	20,696	1,372
High schools (colleges, universities, technical institutes)	26	16,978	1,204	122	96,890	7,916	244	158,010	12,475
Total	10,352	1,708,234	49,925	16,951	2,907,882	120,151	17,878	3,562,220	136,316

Source: Research Department, National Bank of Yugoslavia, and *Statistički godišnjak 1960* and *1963*, pp. 266 (*1960*), 296–301 (*1963*).
* Prewar data for primary and secondary schools are not strictly comparable. Before the war primary schools had four grades and the secondary schools eight grades. Primary schools now have eight grades and secondary schools four.

mendation of the Federal Assembly in 1957. Thenceforth more opportunities were to be provided for the training of highly specialized personnel. Another important step was taken in 1960 with the passage of a general law concerning universities and university faculties and the Resolution of the Federal Assembly concerning occupational training. The effect was to decentralize the educational system. The general law and the Resolution extended the right to establish higher educational units to economic organizations and local authorities. Entry into the universities was to be free provided the applicant could meet prescribed academic standards. Those without the necessary secondary education were to be admitted in special circumstances. As indicated in Table 10, the results were about what one would expect. The

TABLE 10. Distribution of university faculties for selected academic years

University	1938/39	1946/47	1948/49	1954/55	1959/60	1960/61
Belgrade	9	9	15	19	20	23
Zagreb	6	8	9	9	15	18
Ljubljana	4	5	6	13	9	9
Sarajevo	0	2	3	7	9	11
Skopje	1	1	3	5	7	7
Novi Sad	0	0	0	0	0	7
Total	20	25	36	53	60	75 *

Source: "The System of Higher Education," *Yugoslav Survey*, March 1961, p. 529.
* Does not include six detached departments.

number of university faculties in 1960/1961 were 25 per cent higher than those in the academic year 1959/1960.

The country in general, nonetheless, suffers from insufficient social facilities such as schools, housing, roads, and hospitals. Much of the postwar effort has gone into developing industry, so that in effect the economy has been intentionally unbalanced. At times such unbalance threatens to strangle further economic development of the country. Indeed, one of Yugoslavia's principal problems is the extraordinary lack of trained people to run a complex industrial economy. The lack is obvious to even the casual visitor in the country, and the weaknesses in the economy are compounded by the mistakes of the labor force.

4.

THE PRICE SYSTEM, PLANNING, AND ECONOMIC DEVELOPMENT

THE PROBLEM

In this study "economic development" and "economic growth" are assumed to go hand in hand. These concepts are understood to mean expansion in an area's capacity to produce things. Considerable disagreement exists as to the role of the price system and planning in economic development. Some argue that the price system as embodied in a free-market type of economy is incapable of promoting rapid economic development. Others argue that economic planning tends to introduce severe distortions and imbalances as well as bureaucratization into the economy and that these frustrate economic development. This chapter will discuss briefly the role of prices and planning in modern economies.

THE ROLE OF PRICES IN A MARKET ECONOMY

In his book *Economic Organization* Frank Knight points out that the economic problem may be broken down into five interrelated problems.[1] Provision must be made by every society for

---

[1] Chicago: University of Chicago Press, 1933. See also Milton Friedman's "Lectures in Price Theory" (mimeographed, University of Chicago, 1955).

34

handling these five problems: (1) fixing standards, (2) organizing production, (3) distributing the product, (4) providing for economic maintenance, and (5) adjusting consumption to production over short periods.

The existence of alternative ends implies that there must be some way of setting priorities among these ends and resolving conflicting evaluations by individuals within a society. In the free-market type of economy this problem is resolved by voting in the market place with money. Such an arrangement amounts to proportional representation and allows economic minority groups within society to make their desires known. These votes in the free-market type of economy manifest themselves through prices that in turn reflect the standards of society.

The translation of these standards into production among and within industries again involves prices. The task is accomplished by the interaction of two sets of prices: the prices of products and the prices of resources. Prices of products in relation to their costs of production determine the distribution of inputs among industries; the relative prices of input factors, in turn, determine the coordination of these factors within industries.

Some means for dividing the total product must be established by every society. In a society incorporating the free-market type of economy this task is accomplished by the price system. Under such an arrangement separate individuals in a society own the means used in production. They get a claim on society's product by selling services on the market for a price. An individual's total claim on the product is determined by the quantity of resources he owns and the prices at which he can sell all the services of these resources. The return per unit of time of resource or input factor prices in conjunction with the distribution of ownership of resources determines the distribution of the total product among individuals in the society.

In effect, prices serve as signals indicating where economic resources are wanted most and at the same time provide an incentive for people to obey these signals. It is because factor prices serve the function of distributing the product that other prices, mainly product prices, can serve the functions of fixing standards and organizing production.

The first three problems listed above deal with the adjustment of production to consumption. The organization of existing resources and their utilization in known ways are the only economic problems with which a static society need concern itself. In a changing society, however, the problem of affecting the volume of resources and changing the ways in which they can be utilized requires solution. This is the fourth problem in our list, and it concerns economic maintenance and progress. In a free-market type of economy the relevant price for solving this problem is the interest rate, which provides an incentive for owners of capital to maintain their capital or add to it. And here an individual consumer in his savings choice has a voice in decisions affecting economic growth. Some provision must be made for quick adjustment of relatively fixed supplies of a commodity to consumption (the fifth problem). Bribery, chance, favoritism, or prices are among the means available to society to accomplish this task. When free bidding for goods is permitted, prices will adjust themselves so that the quantity people want to buy at the market price is equal to the quantity available.

In solving our five problems prices do three things: they transmit information effectively and efficiently; they provide an incentive to users of resources to follow such information; and they provide an incentive to owners of resources to follow this information.

This summary of the role of prices in a free-market type of economy is a brief and highly oversimplified version of an extremely subtle and highly complex procedure. The complexities are driven home only when something goes wrong or attempts are made to find substitute methods for solving the five interrelated problems.

THE PRICE SYSTEM AND ECONOMIC DEVELOPMENT

Criticism of the price system on the ground that it cannot achieve economic development rests on the relevance of external economies and complementarities.[2] According to this argument private and social benefits differ where economies are external to the firm and to the industry. Where complementary factors and facilities are lacking, economic development is arrested. Industry, for example, is slow to take advantage of relatively low wages in circumstances where complementary facilities are virtually nonexistent.

Though the argument that the price system cannot achieve rapid economic development rests on the existence of external economies, the argument that it will not rests on internal economies and monopoly.[3] For successful operation the price system requires effective competition as an energy source. Otherwise the economy rests on dead center with private enterprise and the price system but makes little economic progress.

Coupled with these arguments is another which draws on the divergence between private and social costs and on the existence of external diseconomies.[4] According to this argument private individuals may be willing to develop a country's natural resources only if they can appropriate the capital represented by these resources.

In defense of the price system the advantages most often cited, at least in well-developed economies, are in the areas of capital formation, dispersal of decisions and risks, and the incentive to innovate.[5] The private entrepreneur usually makes a better collector for capital formation than does the government. Since there is considerable uncertainty as to the exact nature of the bottlenecks impeding economic development, it makes little sense to allocate all of one's resources to a single goal, which may in the final analysis prove unprofitable. New methods and ideas seldom receive a favorable audience in bureaucracies, where there is a tendency to dodge responsibility and cling to old methods and ideas.

As an economy develops and resources acquire mobility so that

---

[2] Charles P. Kindleberger, *Economic Development* (New York: McGraw-Hill, 1958) , p. 132.

[3] *Ibid.,* p. 133.   [4] *Ibid.*   [5] *Ibid.,* p. 134.

demand and supply elasticities become more pronounced, the price system will operate more smoothly, thereby enabling marginal and structural changes to occur in the economy. People with a singular distrust in the operation of the price mechanism tend to behave as though they have a universal mind at their disposal; as a result they may fail to take advantage of the mechanism's contribution as a delicate integrator of complex economic events. The net effect may be a serious retardation in the development of the economy.

Implicit in the "low supply elasticity" argument is the questionable assertion that people in underdeveloped areas have little desire "to make money." Surely it is more accurate to argue that people in these lands tend to be less aware of alternative opportunities. If so, steps should be taken to improve the market's operation through better information instead of turning to an elaborate planning structure "until the elasticities become larger."

With regard to external diseconomies and complementarities, rigid central planners and critics of the price system have overstated their case. Recent work by Ronald H. Coase, for example, suggests possible solutions to these vexing problems within the price system.[6] And James M. Buchanan's work indicates that the imperfections that arise out of political attempts to solve these problems may outweigh the economic benefits.[7] Viewing the world as though it were composed primarily of complements has, moreover, serious methodological drawbacks.[8]

ECONOMIC PLANNING UNDER CAPITALISM

All modern economies tend to be mixed in the sense that they incorporate elements of both the price mechanism and economic planning. The difference, of course, is that some economies incorporate more of the one than the other. The highly centralized and

6 "The Problem of Social Cost," *Journal of Law and Economics*, Oct. 1960, pp. 1–44.

7 "Politics, Policy and the Pigovian Margins," *Economica*, Feb. 1962, pp. 17–24.

8 George Macesich, "Current Inflation Theory: Consideration on Methodology," *Social Research*, Autumn 1961, pp. 321–30.

planned command economy of the Soviet Union still allows an element of private production in agriculture and distribution in response to profit opportunities dictated by free prices. Indeed, even in its nationalized production the Soviet Union uses a system of prices in reaching decisions respecting output and distribution.

Ever since the catastrophic depression of the 1930's, pronounced attempts have been made to mitigate the effects of the operation of free-market types of economies. Such interference in the form of countercyclical monetary and fiscal policies and built-in stabilizers is justified by most economists as assuring relatively high levels of employment and output. These policies and stabilizers have mitigated but not eliminated the business cycle. They have not solved to everyone's satisfaction the problem of economic growth without inflation.

In the United States "planning" on a substantial scale has occurred in the industrial sector only in wartime. During World War II, for example, the production of aircraft and other munitions was thoroughly planned, and the output of civilian goods was curtailed by means of limitation orders, low priorities on materials and manpower, and the direction of critical materials into war-supporting activities.

An unusual peacetime plan was embodied in the Veterans Emergency Housing Program following World War II. Schedules of housing starts were centrally planned, and an attempt was made to implement the housing schedule by means of priorities, material allocations, and limitation orders on "less essential" construction. Subsidies were given to stimulate production of some building materials. Many difficulties were encountered in scheduling, chiefly because it was difficult to admit that a highly publicized schedule was not being met. Unrealistic scheduling with attendant misallocations of materials and other resources tended to ensue.[9]

Since World War II some countries with hitherto relatively free economies have sought a solution to the problem of economic

[9] This is described and analyzed in detail in M. R. Colberg, "Federal Control of Construction Following World War II" (unpublished doctoral dissertation, University of Michigan, 1950), chap. iv.

growth by nationalizing certain industries considered by them to be important but privately neglected sources of economic growth. By the 1950's, however, it was discovered that nationalization was not the way out and its popularity began to ebb. In Great Britain, for example, old-style socialists received a serious setback when British Conservatives beat the Laborites in 1953 and denationalized the steel industry.

More recently attention has been focused on the European continent and on so-called indicative planning in market economies. The object of this interest is the "French Plan" and its indicative planning.[10] The purpose apparently is to give the capitalist type of economy a "sense of direction" by indicating to business what investment outlets appear to be best from the long-run viewpoint of the total economy. At the same time, this method of planning, according to its supporters, serves to encourage governmental concern over long-term growth as well as short-term stability in the economy.

Economic research joins with programing as the basic techniques of the French Plan. Coupled with these techniques is a series of conferences with leading industrial leaders and others, the aim of which is apparently to get the businessmen to talk each other into a concerted viewpoint and action. The programing technique is Wassily W. Leontief's input-output system whereby it is indicated what every major sector of the economy including the government must do to attain a national growth objective. According to its French sponsors, the input-output system is nothing more than a contract on a national scale and hence easily understood by businessmen.

Unless active cooperation between businessmen and government is achieved, the French system of planning has little chance for the realization of its objectives. In order to get such cooperation, the French sell the idea to both that it is in effect their plan.

The building of the current French Four-Year-Plan, 1962–65,

---

[10] "Europe Charts Its Business Future," *Business Week*, April 7, 1962, pp. 80–92.

took more than a year and occurred in four stages. The first stage was essentially the government's for its technicians sketched a plan for over-all investment, labor requirements, gross national product, exports, imports, consumption, and governmental spending for three possible annual rates of economic growth, namely 3 per cent, 4½ per cent, and 6 per cent. The second stage involved a broader discussion of the plan with representatives of government, labor, industry, consumers, and other interested groups. The result of these discussions was a decision to attempt to reach a 5 per cent rate of annual growth. On the basis of this decision the government's experts drew up another plan to provide for a 5 per cent rate of growth. In the third stage the new 5 per cent plan went to a group of twenty-five committees and their subcommittees; there it was corrected with two objectives in mind: first, to verify its technical assumptions regarding labor, investment, and domestic and foreign market prospects; second, to work out expansion plans for individual enterprises. The fourth stage combined the industry reports and the government's tentative plan with a new target rate of annual growth of 5½ per cent. Approved and amended by the French government, the plan serves as a guide to economic policy.

Adoption by the French government does not necessarily compel the government and other participants to execute the plan. Psychological coercion is insufficient to bind the participants, though it is helpful in that the participants are unlikely to disengage themselves from a plan that they helped to create. A much more powerful incentive toward cooperation is the fact that the French government is in large measure in control of the capital market. France's four big banks are nationalized, and they control more than half of the country's bank deposits. In addition, the government provides 26 per cent of all investment capital for private industry. Moreover, no enterprise in France can issue debenture capital unless it has the approval of the government. A normal requirement for such approval is that the issues be consistent with the plan. Coupled with these inducements to cooperate is the fact that the government through its nationalized industries such as transportation and utilities possesses a third of all of the country's productive investment.

The importance of the French system of planning to the Common Market is clear. The West Germans, for example, though at first cool toward the idea of open planning, are now beginning to express more than lukewarm enthusiasm. According to European supporters of French planning, the current German reaction comes as no surprise. The so-called German Miracle, they argue, is largely due to the fact that from 1948 to 1957 56 per cent of the net investment was financed by the West German government directly or indirectly (chiefly through direct loans to industry and by tax exemptions) rather than to the operation of a free-market economy.[11] Even the British have now set up a planning council with the slogan, "Conservative planning pays."

The important question to be raised is whether the planning philosophy current in the Common Market will not ultimately degenerate into totalitarian capitalism or fascism. The current stumbling steps away from the free market may prove to be the first taken in that general direction. In appearance totalitarian capitalism or fascism is similar to capitalism in that it "superficially maintains private property in the means of production, has essentially the same income distribution as the private enterprise system, and maintains, on paper, the same economic freedoms to consume and to work together with private initiative and competition." [12] The difference, of course, is that such an organization implies a collectivist plan wherein so-called social aims always take precedence over the private ends of individuals. On this score General de Gaulle's design for a new France to be constructed by "all the vital elements" of the state has a remarkably familiar ring. It sounds like the proposals heard in the grim 1930's and 40's.[13] If these observations prove to be correct, the current supporters of a

[11] *Ibid.*, p. 81.
[12] George Halm, *Economic Systems* (New York: Holt, Rinehart, and Winston, 1960) , p. 166.
[13] "Europe Charts Its Business Future," p. 86.

new Europe and French planning may well be contributing to a world of government-supported cartels and international trade restrictions instead of to competition, which most people associate with the Common Market.

ECONOMIC PLANNING UNDER SOCIALISM

The essential difference between socialism and capitalism is that socialism entails public ownership and management of the bulk of the material means of production. Although the cause of economic planning is advanced in the name of economic growth and development by socialists and some capitalists, the former have at least a greater distrust than the latter in what they consider to be the "blind forces" of the market and in the decisions of people who can only see a small part of the total economic picture.

Even socialists, however, do not agree on the role of economic planning in the economy. Some argue for rigid central planning, while others temper such planning with relative consumer sovereignty and freedom of occupational choice. In economic literature one of the most sophisticated exponents of the later approach to socialist planning has been Oskar Lange.[14] The critical issue is that adherence to consumer sovereignty as a guide to production precludes central planning.[15] Advocates of this approach are obliged to show how central planning can be reconciled with consumer sovereignty and how consistent pricing is compatible with artificial markets where public managers deal almost exclusively among themselves. The problem of cost calculation and factor allocation in such an economy is indeed of the first magnitude. If it is impossible to maintain an adequate pricing process in such an economy, the guidance of production by consumers is impossible. Central authority will have to rule, as in the case of rigid central planning, by direct decision.

An attempt to solve the pricing problem in such an economy has

[14] "On the Economic Theory of Socialism," in B. E. Lippincott, ed., *Economic Theory of Socialism* (Minneapolis: University of Minnesota Press, 1948) , pp. 55–143.
[15] Halm, *op. cit.*, p. 482.

been made by Lange. His argument, in effect, is that prices can be determined by the same process of trial and error by which they are determined in the unplanned, competitive market type of economy. According to Lange, the trial and error method is based on the "parametric function of prices." [16] To illustrate his point Lange argues that central planners can start such a process with a given set of prices chosen at random, though in practice the trial and error method would be based on historically given prices. All that is required is that producers and consumers make their decisions based on these prices. As a result the quantities of each commodity supplied and demanded would be determined. In the event that the quantity supplied was not equal to the quantity demanded, the price would have to be changed by the central planners, who would then raise the price if the quantity supplied fell short of the quantity demanded, and conversely. The central planners would fix new prices which would serve as a basis for new decisions and which would result in a new set of quantities demanded and supplied. Equilibrium prices would finally be established through this process of trial and error.

Lange's proposals have been attacked by both advocates of a free-market economy and advocates of rigid central planning. The former argue that such a system of artificial pricing would not obtain desired results because it neglects the profit motive and competition, which are the mainsprings of a market economy. The latter argue against the trial and error method on the ground that it implies such a degree of decentralization that planned action is rendered almost useless.

In addition to their important role in the pricing process, central planners under Lange's proposal would have the task of setting the rate of accumulation and in effect determining the division between the production of consumer goods and investment goods. Another important task delegated to them would be the allocation of investment funds among competing ends. Such allocations would be based, presumably, on parametric interest

[16] Lange, *op. cit.*, p. 86.

rates established and continually adjusted by the central planning organization to reflect underlying supply and demand conditions for capital funds.

Detailed production instructions would not be given to the various enterprises by central planners. And the reason, of course, is that the planners lack the detailed knowledge to meet on-the-spot conditions. Contrary to the pretensions of central planners, universal knowledge is not at their fingertips.

Rigid central planners, on the other hand, argue that their central planning organization would be more than simply a price-fixing agency.[17] It is the investment problem and not the problem of consumer preferences that is important. The irrational behavior of an unplanned economy, according to rigid central planners, can be attributed to investment decisions made by many independent units. The centralization of investment decision makes rigid central planning all but inevitable.

Paul M. Sweezy, for example, provides us with an illustration of what the central planning organization would attempt to undertake.[18] Once a government has decided on how much of the national income to invest and establishes the objectives of such investment, the central planning organization would undertake the drawing up of an investment plan for the execution of these objectives. When the investment plan was completed and the various material and labor requirements were estimated, the consumption schedules would be consolidated with the available economic resources to carry out the total economic plan for the period under consideration. Once adopted there would be little alternative for individual enterprises but to conform with the requirements of the economic plan. The very minor and subservient role played by the price system coupled with the centralization of decision-making powers in a central planning authority stands in marked contrast to the looser planning apparatus espoused by Lange.

---

[17] Halm, *op. cit.*, p. 221, and Paul M. Sweezy, *Socialism* (New York: McGraw-Hill, 1949).

[18] *Op. cit.*

Rigid central planning rests on several premises that deserve discussion.[19] The first is that consumer sovereignty can and should be abolished. Though consumer goods may be distributed through the market, there is no reason for consumers to direct production. The second is that the choice among alternative production methods is far less formidable than economic literature supposes it to be. Historical, technological, and social factors limit the productive choice to manageable proportions. The third is that the longer the planning period the greater the number of possible investment patterns. These plans cannot be made by independent producing units since they rest on parallel developments of interdependent industries. The fourth is that economic development through long-range planning is far more important than the question of how a perfect static equilibrium can be reached. The fifth is that constant checking of the internal consistency of the plan can be accomplished by "balances," so that equilibrium in the development process can be accomplished. The sixth is that these balances provide a means whereby the interrelationships of the different industries are known and planned *ex ante* rather then in the *ex post* manner of a market economy. Continual checking of the plan is required as it is carried out.

Implicit in these premises is the assertion that complementarity rather than substitution is dominant in the economy. Such an assertion oversimplifies the problem confronting central planners.[20] As Maurice Dobb writes, "The items which compose consumers' aggregate demand to any large extent form a closely interrelated set, bound together, e.g., by social convention or by links of complementarity between particular wants into 'modes of life' or patterns of behavior which assume the character of organic wholes." [21]

There may be some truth in this view, however little, for underdeveloped countries that are too poor for the issue of choice to have significant operational meaning. With development and

<hr>

[19] For an extended discussion of these premises, see Halm, *op. cit.*, pp. 225 ff.

[20] It also leads to serious theoretical difficulties (Macesich, *op. cit.*, p. 327) .

[21] *Soviet Economic Development since 1917* (New York: International Publishers, 1948) , p. 15.

the satisfaction of so-called basic wants the issue of consumer choice does begin to have some economic meaning. At this stage of development the consumer presumably is less willing to accept the compromises of his sovereignty required by central planners.

The argument that a more standardized demand resulting from a more equal distribution of income would simplify the planners' problems overlooks the important point that people with relatively similar incomes have widely varying tastes. Moreover, such equality in income distribution tends to conflict with the maintenance of freedom in choosing an occupation.[22] Wage differentials must of necessity exist if labor is to be attracted to various occupations. And if these wage differentials are to be more than window dressing, they must be convertible into claims against society's income.

The second premise of central planning is also subject to question. Unless we are speaking of a world of strict complementarity, changes in production patterns can be brought about even in the very short run. All sorts of changes are possible and do occur. Central planners may choose to act as if they lived in a one-commodity world. Such an assumption would simplify their problem, but it would not eliminate reality. Presumably the centrally planned economy would technically resemble the advanced free-market economy, and if so it would be necessary to incorporate in some way the changing circumstances confronting the economy.

The third premise is the one most often cited in favor of planning because it would effectively eliminate uncertainty by substituting *ex ante* coordination in the economic plan for *ex post* coordination via the market place. This of course supposes that central planners possess and effectively use more information than is available to individual producing units. Unfortunately there is always a tendency for such planning groups to degenerate into bureaucracies, which may be unable, or indeed unwilling, to act on the basis of such additional information.

The fourth premise argues in fact that the real test of an

---

[22] For a contrary view, see Lange, *op. cit.*, p. 102.

economic system as a contributor to human welfare is its ability to develop successfully from one situation to another. According to this view, the planned economy is superior because it is not obsessed with the free-market notion of an optimum allocation of resources among competing ends with both resources and uses taken as given. The reply, of course, is that even a centrally planned economy cannot dispense with the concept of equilibrium. All social economies must attempt to reach positions wherein they make the most of their available resources. Scarce resources must be distributed among competing ends in the most efficient manner if the economy is to avoid bottlenecks and economic breakdown. There is nothing in the nature of economic planning to suggest that its institution would have the effect of removing the difficult problem involved in the efficient allocation of resources or to substitute for the useful concept of economic equilibrium in reaching such a solution.

The fifth and sixth premises and their succession of approximations appear at first glance to resemble the way in which equilibrium is reached in a market economy. The plan grows to perfection, as it were, in a series of trials and errors during which the initial distortions of general policy decisions are eliminated by various experts. The difference between this approach and that in the market type of economy, however, is that in the centrally planned economy the correction of distortions is concerned only with the removal of them within the framework of the plan. Such corrections do not overrule the central decision makers.

The most telling criticism against rigid central planning is the wide and embarrassing gap between theory and practice. A prominent Yugoslav economist, Rudolf Bićanić, has put the severity of its shortcomings in this way:

To those who have lived under a system of centralized bureaucratic, normative planning, its expense in human and economic terms and the damage which it can do at all levels of economy are obvious. Sometimes people . . . are led astray by the bias for rationalization to the superficial assumption that centralization means greater efficiency and greater speed. The balancing of supply and demand in a centrally planned economy occurs in offices where a few people, unaware of the real effects of their authoritarian plans, become the supreme judges of the destinies of all producers and consumers through their bureaucratic machine.[23]

Professor Bićanić's comments on central planning stand in marked contrast to those of such theoretical advocates as Professor Sweezy.

The Soviets apparently believe that many of the shortcomings inherent in rigid central planning can be reduced if not eliminated by the use of high-speed computers. It has been reported that a Soviet computing center has worked out a three-year plan for the country which required 360,000,000 electronic operations.[24] How successful such high-speed electronic computers as the Soviet Ural 2 and Ural 4 will be in serving as substitutes for the "free-market computer" remains to be demonstrated.

[23] "Economic Growth under Centralized and Decentralized Planning: Yugoslavia a Case Study," *Economic Development and Cultural Change,* Oct. 1957, p. 66; also quoted in Albert Waterston, "Planning in Yugoslavia" (MS, 1962), p. 16.

[24] *New York Times,* April 14, 1963, p. 32.

5.

ECONOMIC PLANNING
AND THE PRICE SYSTEM:
THE YUGOSLAV SYNTHESIS

THE CHANGING ROLE OF ECONOMIC PLANNING

Yugoslavia in the 1950's was one of the few countries that could claim relative success in carrying out its development programs via a novel synthesis of economic planning, a price system, and a sizable private sector within a basically unchanged political system. The dismantling of the rigid Soviet-type central planning apparatus after 1952 ushered in a period of trial and error in planning that is still incomplete. Current economic planning in the country can perhaps be best described as comparable to the economic budgeting based on national income analysis used in some Western countries.[1] The plan rests on analyses of past economic trends and forecasts together with targets established by the Federal Assembly. It provides, in effect, a framework for the future development of the economy. Such development is facilitated by provisions that are sufficiently flexible, apparently, to take into account changes in the basic forces underlying supply and demand. In order to create a favorable climate for the execution of the

[1] Janez Stanovnik, "Planning through the Market," *Foreign Affairs*, Jan. 1962, p. 255.

plan, built-in economic incentives are reinforced by monetary and fiscal measures.

An example of how Yugoslav planning since decentralization has taken firm hold is provided in the country's annual plan for 1962. The plan, covering twenty-five pages in the *Official Gazette*, is divided into four parts.[2] The first part presents a short statement of the basic purposes and objectives of the plan; the second contains a statement of proposed directions for the development of the economy that includes broad quantitative estimates of national output and income, investment, consumption, standard of living, employment, productivity, and international trade, as well as federal expenditures for defense, administration, and other categories of noninvestment expenditures; estimated volume and value of the output by sectors; and an outline of economic instruments that are to be employed in the execution of the plan.

Some idea of the differences between past and current planning practice is indicated by the fact that before 1952, when centralized planning was in force, the completed annual plan weighed over 3,300 pounds.[3] Over 215 ministers on the federal and republic levels were issuing orders to enterprises, and the Federal Planning Commission employed a staff of 700 people. The amount of paper work imposed on the enterprises is indicated by the fact that each year they were required to submit from 600 to 800 reports to the central authorities. Daily reports were required from enterprises, and these were then telegraphed at the end of each work day by the local authorities to the appropriate ministries in Belgrade. These ministries would then consolidate their reports and send them along to the Federal Planning Commission.

Various people and groups checked on the execution of the plan and on the efficiency of the enterprises. These might be roaming federal inspectors or individual citizen groups that zealously sought out what they considered to be shortcomings of enterprises. To add to the general confusion, production was often impeded

---

[2] Albert Waterston, "Planning in Yugoslavia" (MS, 1962), p. 40.

[3] *Ibid.*, p. 12.

when officials and ministries failed to provide instructions on time or issued contradictory instructions.

Most of the shortcomings of rigid central planning made their appearance in one form or another before 1952, and the effects of these shortcomings are still visible in the economy. The replacement of consumer sovereignty and most of the price system by *ex ante* coordination ushered in the grandiose first Five-Year Plan for 1947–51. The operation of the plan was cut short by the political events of 1948 that resulted in the Cominform blockade and by the two severe droughts of 1950 and 1952. There is thus no way of ascertaining accurately what to some appear to be the central planners' overestimates of the economy's ability to carry out the plan. Such evidence as is available suggests that more zeal than technical knowledge went into the plan's formulation. Enterprise managers overestimated their production potentials. These errors were later compounded by central planners in the belief that under central planning an even higher output was possible.

The argument that the limiting influences of factor supply and technical know-how limit the practical choices open to central planners and so facilitate their task is erroneous. The limited resources increase the importance of making correct choices and make more difficult *ex ante* coordination. Cost estimates provided the planners under the first Five-Year Plan were later proved to be inaccurate because of the inexperience of those submitting proposals or because of fear that particular projects would be neglected because their estimates were too high. The result was to produce an inaccurate choice of projects on the part of planners which led to waste and inefficiency.

These errors were further compounded by the inability of planners accurately to forecast the production of complementary factors. And it is precisely on the issue of complementarity that planners tend to base their arguments. From the supply side they seriously underestimated the time necessary to increase the supply of such a critical factor as the skilled labor force that would be required for the new industries. Indeed, there was an insufficient number of skilled people to operate even the country's modest

1946 industrial establishment; hence when new capacity was added to the economy, it was insufficiently utilized.

From the demand side they fumbled with the solution to the problem of complementarities among industries, especially in the area of the relation between agriculture and industry. In order to increase agricultural output resort was had to low investments, low prices for compulsory deliveries, and high prices for goods which farmers bought. These actions together with a policy of forced collectivization of agriculture reduced agricultural output to below its prewar level. To further complicate matters the plan called for sizable increases in the export of raw materials at the same time that the country's domestic requirements for these materials expanded.

An escape from problems arising out of internal supply is provided in foreign trade. The planners, however, underestimated the amount of foreign exchange that would be required to carry out the plan. In addition, the large-scale aid that they counted on from the Cominform countries was not forthcoming. Expensive foundations were laid for machinery which never arrived.

The absence of a comprehensive and consistent pricing system blurred the importance of opportunity costs and led to such practices as allocating grants from the federal budget without any obligation to repay. The result was a scramble for grants by various local authorities that is reminiscent of the American "Distribution of the Surplus Revenue in 1837." [4] Funds were used to construct plants that often needlessly duplicated existing capacity.

Lack of adequate cost criteria and insistence on output targets led managers of enterprises to achieve these targets at no matter what the cost. Constant meddling in the internal affairs of enterprises by various groups did little to lighten the burden of harassed managers. The results were about what one would expect: incorrect factor "mixes," shortages, products of inferior quality, the compounding of errors, a stifling of initiative on the part of the

[4] George Macesich, "Sources of Monetary Disturbances in the United States, 1834–45," *Journal of Economic History*, Sept. 1960, pp. 407–34.

producers, and in general a demoralization of both producers and consumers.

Contrary to the arguments of some people, central planning does not eliminate monopoly exploitation of consumers. If anything it encourages such exploitation. Thus Professor Rudolf Bićanić observes,

> One can scarcely look with nostalgia upon the times when the entire city of Zagreb . . . was supplied by a single large retail business enterprise and one consumers' cooperative, and when in 1947, the largest beaches on the Adriatic Coast were entitled to no more than one type of cake a day in all restaurants, cafes, and bakeries. . . . The monopoly of an industry by one firm for one product was achieved as in a treatise of political economy, but the cakes were not very appetizing. Today the savings of large-scale production are less, but the cakes better.[5]

The problem is not simply to increase output but to satisfy consumer wants, and it would appear that the tastes and preferences of central planners seldom coincide with those of the general consumer.

The argument that central planning degenerates into a stifling bureaucracy is adequately supported by Yugoslav experience. As Professor Gerškovič writes, "During the few years of building socialism in Yugoslavia the harmful effects of such a system have been shown up. Wherever bureaucratic centralism appeared it put a brake on initiative. Wherever inflexible, bureaucratic, centralistic planning reared its head, there was disorder in production and distribution." [6] It would appear that the Yugoslavs have recognized that economic development is far too important to be left in bureaucratic hands.

The problem of capital accumulation is in effect the same in all economic systems. Basically it amounts to resolving the issue of how much to cut down the possible present consumption level and

---

[5] Rudolf Bićanić, "La Concurrence socialiste en Yougoslavie," *Économie appliquée, Archives de l'Institut de Science Économique Appliquée* (Paris), July–Sept. 1956, p. 343.

[6] As reported by Waterston, *op. cit.*, p. 16.

how much to save in order to raise the standard of living in the future by increased production of capital goods. A basic truth in economics is that irrespective of the system involved it is impossible to allocate all available resources to the production of capital goods.

It is asserted that a centralized planning system has the advantage of being able to marshal substantial rates of investment. And indeed Yugoslavia during its centralized period was able to marshal for investment annually over a quarter of its national income. If these figures are correct, such investment rates undoubtedly helped to lay the material foundations for later development.

The marshaling of investment funds is only one part of the problem—albeit an important part. The other part involves the allocation of these funds among competing projects. Regardless of the type of economic system, it is imperative that investment funds be put to the best possible use with reference to the aims of the economy. In the free-market type of economy the interest rate is the relevant price for distributing these funds among competing ends.

There is reason to believe that during their heyday central planners in Yugoslavia tended to disregard the importance of the interest rate and the help that it would have given to them in solving the problem of investment allocation. Simple reference to a plan is insufficient because it only leads to the question of how the plan can be designed so as to achieve the most efficient allocation of investment funds. Attempts to solve this problem without the use of interest rates complicate the already difficult task confronting the planners. Use of interest rates would not have compromised the authority of central planners. Indeed, this use of interest rates would have made it easier for them to choose rationally, would have facilitated the translation of their objectives into production plans, and would have solved the problem of the selection of the proper capital intensity for different production processes. Disregard of interest rates resulted in a desire on the part of the economy for such capital intensity that the technological utopia implied became an absurdity.

External political events combined with the severe drought of 1950 forced the government to replace the Five-Year Plan with a more modest Key Investment Program. Far less ambitious, the program eliminated many of the projects called for by the Five-Year Plan. It called for concentration on transport, power and fuel, and other projects that would eliminate serious bottlenecks and have favorable effects on the balance of payments. Owing to the uncertainty created by the Eastern bloc and the difficult position occupied by Yugoslavia, it was not until the end of 1956 that the program was completed.[7]

SCOPE AND METHOD OF ECONOMIC PLANNING

If official pronouncements are to be taken seriously, the principal objectives of economic planning in Yugoslavia are the attainment of the highest possible rate of economic growth together with the highest possible increase in the real standard of living. To achieve these objectives planning encompasses three types of economic plans. They are classified according to the time periods covered, such as annual plans, medium-term or five-year plans, and long-term or fifteen-twenty-year plans. These plans are formulated on the federal, republic, and local levels of government as well as by various economic enterprises with apparently a considerable degree of freedom of action on the part of all concerned. A five-year plan will serve the purposes of illustration.

A brief summary of the targets set up for the 1961–65 plan is useful in understanding the scope and method of five-year economic planning. According to estimates presented by Branko Kubović and Vidosav Tričković, the total national income is to grow at a rate of 11 per cent and per capita income at 9.6 per cent.[8] Such rates are higher than those achieved in the period 1953–59, when the total national income grew at 9.4 per cent and per capita income at 7.9 per cent.

The mainsprings of this growth are to be industry and agri-

[7] *Ibid.*, p. 15.
[8] *National and Regional Economic Planning in Yugoslavia* (Belgrade: Federal Planning Bureau, 1961), p. 23.

culture, with total industrial output expected to increase by 85 per cent and agricultural output by 50 per cent. This does not mean that various branches of industry will increase their outputs at the same rates. Some are expected to grow faster than others, as for example the chemical, equipment, food-processing, and construction industries. Expansion of agricultural output, which is a particularly thorny problem, is expected to be facilitated by strengthening voluntary cooperatives, thereby permitting better and more fruitful cooperation between private farmers and the socialist sector.

The standard of living is expected to undergo marked improvement, with total consumption increasing by 50 per cent and on a per capita basis by 40 per cent. The composition of consumption is expected to change with increases in personal incomes. The proportion of total consumer expenditures on food is expected to decline. This decline is supposed to be replaced by greater expenditures on income-elastic products such as durable and semidurable consumer goods and meat products, whose consumption is expected to increase by 50 per cent.

Expenditures for health, housing, and education are to increase by 80 per cent or by about 13 per cent annually. Together with increases in personal consumption the "total living standard" is to rise by about 9.5 per cent, approximating the rate at which national income is to grow.

Such changes in the economy are expected to bring about continuing socioeconomic changes in the character of the population. Increases in employment in the socialist sector averaging 200,000 people annually will continue to decrease the proportion of the agricultural population to the total population from 50 per cent in 1960 to 41 per cent in 1965.

The drafting of annual, five-year, and long-term plans on the federal level is the responsibility of the Federal Planning Bureau. On a particular level of government whether republic, district, or commune, the drafting of plans is the responsibility of the planning agencies of that level. Figure 1 illustrates the relations of various agencies concerned with planning.

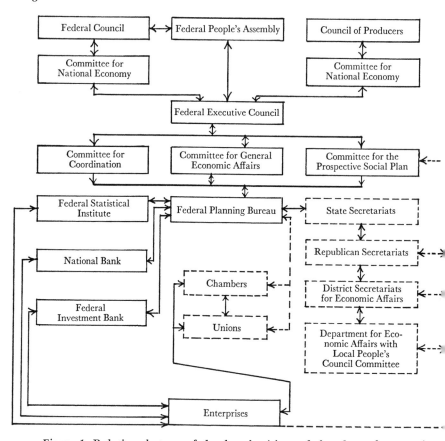

Figure 1. Relations between federal authorities and the plans of economic enterprise. Solid lines = primary relations; broken lines = secondary relations. (Adapted from B. Kubović and V. Tričković, *National and Regional Economic Planning in Yugoslavia* [Belgrade: Federal Planning Bureau, 1961].)

In drafting a plan, the federal organization receives active cooperation from planning agencies at various levels of government as well as from other organizations and groups such as the National Bank, the Secretariats for Industry, Agriculture, Trade, and Finance, Economic and Producers' Chambers, the Union of General Cooperatives, and research institutes.

Upon completion of the first draft of the plan it is submitted to the Committee for Economic Plans of the Federal Assembly for further discussion. Revisions and adjustments resulting from these discussions are incorporated into the plan by the committee, after which the plan is submitted to the Federal Assembly for consideration. The Assembly may further alter the plan before it is passed.

In order to fulfill the basic objectives of economic planning, technicians in the Federal Planning Bureau attempt to ascertain what in fact are the "highest" rate of economic growth and "highest" level in the standard of living that the economy is capable of achieving. Studies of past performance together with sector and industry analyses and quantitative appraisals of factors believed to be responsible for past economic growth are conducted by the bureau. In these studies particular attention is paid to the past and present results of investment policy as indicated by the proportion of productive and unproductive investment in the total national product and the capital output ratio.[9]

Upon completion of the preliminary analysis, work on building the five-year plan proceeds in three principal steps.[10] First, a general model is built. Second, tentative projections for individual sectors are made. Third, the tentative projections are checked, balanced, and readjusted among the various sectors. The first draft of the plan is then completed and submitted for consideration to the relevant organizations discussed above.

The first step provides a general framework and first approximation to the expected rate of growth of the national product, expected changes in the share of total gross investment in the national product, proportions and rates of growth of personal consumption and social services, and tentative rates of growth for the country's two principal sectors, industry and agriculture. Thus these projections appear to be little more than simple extrapolations of past experience. Insofar as is possible, account is taken of changing circumstances confronting the economy.

The second step makes use of the information provided by the

[9] *Ibid.*, p. 5.
[10] *Ibid.*, pp. 5 ff.

first step to make detailed projections for individual sectors and industries. The method employed takes the form of so-called material balancing. In effect, the method amounts to an intersector input-output table in physical terms and arranged in the form of a rectangular matrix comprising about five hundred individual products and groups of products.

In conjunction with the second step extensive demand studies are conducted for about 70 consumer and investment goods and services. For this purpose foreign as well as domestic experience serves as a guide. For example, the results of international studies of the structure of consumption at different real income levels are used when it is felt that domestic experience does not provide a satisfactory guide for future development.

The checking, balancing, and readjusting of the various sector and industry projections that take place in the third step occur in both physical and value terms. In physical terms material balances are made for about five hundred products and groups of products indicating the amounts to be obtained domestically or imported. Similarly a balance for the total labor force and by skills is made together with recommendations on how to obtain the required skilled manpower. Investment is balanced between fixed and working capital in value terms. So too is personal consumption, which is linked to personal income, estimated consumers' expenditures, and the value of goods and services estimated to be available for meeting the demand. Throughout the third step, the price implications of the expected demand-and-supply conditions are considered, and price elasticities derived from regression studies are employed. Other than for consumer goods such elasticity studies are only now beginning to be taken seriously.

In view of the importance of quantitative studies in guiding the country's economy one would expect considerable data to exist. And indeed numerous data do exist for the derivation of the necessary parameters. These data are provided mainly by the federal and republican statistical institutes, the National Bank, and the investment banks. Various other organizations and groups provide additional data. Unfortunately, no matter how many data and what their quality, the planning mechanism always thirsts for more and better data. And as will be discussed in subsequent chapters, some of the available data leave much to be desired. It is very unlikely that in the near future either in Yugoslavia or the United States data will be available in such quantity and quality as to reduce appreciably the guesswork that too often labels many quantitative studies as little more than interesting exercises. This is particularly true for such ambitious undertakings as the building of input-output tables.[11] Extreme caution coupled with a good dose of skepticism is perhaps the first step toward economic sophistication.

Consider now economic planning below the federal level. Planning agencies are attached to the republic, district, and commune levels of government because each of these levels has the right to formulate its own economic plans. It is important to note that planning agencies, whether on the federal or local levels, have no right to interfere directly with the course of economic events. The right to manage the country's resources belongs exclusively to the "representative bodies of economic organization." [12] Moreover, the planning agencies at the various levels of government are presumably all equal in authority. The agency at the federal level, for example, cannot issue direct orders to those at the lower levels of government. On the other hand, agencies at the lower levels are free to formulate their own plans within the framework of the federal plan. The degree of freedom permitted these agencies as well as enterprises is indicated by the fact that no person or enterprise is held legally accountable for fulfilling any target of the federal plans.[13]

The plans of the several republics differ from the federal plan in that they do not concern themselves directly with foreign trade and general economic trends. Although these plans are formulated within the framework of the federal plans, this does not mean that

[11] George Macesich, "Joint Economic Committee and Inflation," *Social Research*, Autumn 1962, pp. 357–79.

[12] Kubović and Tričković, *op. cit.*, p. 27.

[13] Waterston, *op. cit.*, p. 34.

the republics are under any legal obligation to tailor their plans to fit the federal plan. Realism forces them to pay more than lip service to federal aspirations since the federal plan provides for the distribution of most of the economy's resources. If, however, the republics have additional resources and they are willing to guarantee the achievement of higher goals with the resources made available to them by the federal plan, there is very little that the federal authorities can do to dissuade them.

Much more significant than the plans of the republics and, as elsewhere noted, gaining in importance are the plans of the communes. Although concerned with many of the same issues as the federal and republic plans, the commune plans are much more detailed in supervising strictly local matters and those areas of the economy over which the communes have been given a large measure of responsibility such as commerce, board and lodging services, handicrafts, public utilities, schools, housing construction, health, urban planning, and cultural activities. They also play a significant role in determining the distribution of federal and other investment funds. As already noted, the communes are responsible for organizing and starting new economic enterprises within their areas. Economic enterprises depend heavily on the communes in formulating their plans regarding the output and investment that they will undertake.

As in the republics some measure of control over the communes is exercised by the federal authorities via investment resources and measures designed to achieve the objectives of the federal plan. By and large, however, the communes constitute an important and powerful component of the Yugoslav economy, and they are rapidly replacing the various republics in power and influence. According to the Yugoslavs, these developments are consistent with their rejection of the "fundamental law of socialism" which is practiced in the Soviet Union and other countries and which states that central control of the economy is necessary. On the contrary, they argue that "a central economic plan can never forecast all the details and complicated mutual relations of the entire process of production, the use of all producing capacities and reserves, the needs of consumption, etc." [14]

Economic planning on the enterprise level is formulated independently of any governmental agency. Considerable attention, however, is paid by enterprises to the plans of the various levels of the government, especially to those of the communes. Other organizations advise and guide "the formulation of the plans of economic enterprises" in order that the plans may approximate the objectives laid out by the various levels of government. In addition, legal regulations governing the enterprises, such as those pertaining to the distribution of income, help resolve the often conflicting aims of enterprise and federal plans. So long as these regulations are obeyed, there is very little that government agencies can do to interfere with the freedom of enterprises to plan and operate as they see fit.

The independent plans of the economic enterprises are provisional even after adoption and deal in considerable detail with such items as production, investment, employment, and the distribution of income. They are not required by either law or any government agency to set any fixed output, investment, or employment levels. Neither are they required to submit reports on the fulfillment of their plans, since, in the final analysis, they are guided in their operations by market conditions.

PLANNING AND THE MARKET

Yugoslav critics of central planning on the one hand and the free market on the other can be summarized briefly.[15] Central planning, according to their view, leaves very little initiative to the individual to make the best possible use of available resources. Demand and hence the structure of production are centrally determined by planners. Under these circumstances enterprises are stimulated to overfulfill the plan by the payment of bonuses and not by additional demand. If the planned demand has been a

14 *Ibid.*
15 Stanovnik, *op. cit.*, p. 253.

correct estimate, the stimulation received by the enterprises will upset the balance between supply and demand. In addition, preference given to producer goods is raised to a "basic law of economic development," with the inevitable result of underrating consumer demand and thus limiting the freedom of consumer choice. The free market, according to the Yugoslavs, does not ensure accelerated economic development because its low level of demand does not provide sufficient stimulus for the development of key industries. The profit motive in an underdeveloped economy fails to allocate resources in such a way as to create adequate industrial capacity automatically.

The problem confronting the Yugoslavs, as they see it, is how much consumer sovereignty is compatible with planning, which they view as an important factor in promoting a rapid rate of economic growth. In effect, they are searching for the proper market-planning mix that will yield the most rapid rate of economic growth and at the same time be consistent with the country's institutional framework and the political objectives underlying the "creation of socialism."

According to their view, free-market prices perform two principal functions. They indicate the efficiency of production and they serve as allocators of resources. The first function, they argue, should be maintained and increased. The consumer should be left free to cast his vote according to his preferences for various goods and services, thereby indicating to all concerned his evaluation of the economy's efforts. As to the second, they have reservations. Allocating resources solely according to prices determined by the market may not be desirable because individual and community interests may diverge. According to the Yugoslav interpretation, this divergency does not mean abandoning the market per se. It means that various methods should be developed for influencing the market so that it will behave in a way thought to be in the "community's interest," especially in regard to achieving a rapid rate of economic growth.

If my interpretation of past events is correct, efforts to influence the economy via the market have been growing, though haltingly.

Detailed planning of the 1947–52 type was abandoned and up to 1957 replaced by annual planning as a way of guiding the economy. Through these annual plans the importance of physical planning (subordinating the role of prices) was reduced and the idea of operating through the market gained momentum.[16] Administrative interference with the economy continued in certain sectors considered to be of critical importance by the country's administration. The second Five-Year Plan (1957–61) and especially the third Five-Year Plan (1961–65) ended physical planning and direct administrative interference. This trend was reinforced by the foreign exchange reform of 1961, which eliminated the complex set of multiple exchange rates and established a single exchange rate at 750 dinars to one dollar. These reforms will be discussed separately.

Price controls in various forms still exist. Their existence is justified by the authorities on the ground that such controls facilitate the attainment of the objectives of planning and also eliminate the monopolistic practices of some producers.[17] But, as will be discussed in a subsequent chapter, other reasons may be equally valid. There are guaranteed prices for wheat and corn; these are manipulated so as to stimulate production of these commodities. Various "agreed-upon" prices exist between agriculture and industry. There are also "contract prices," primarily for agricultural raw materials such as sugar beets, oil seeds, and cotton. The intent of these price-setting operations is to stimulate output, taking into account changes in underlying supply-and-demand conditions.

In the nonagricultural field ceiling prices exist for some 30 per cent of the industrially produced raw materials and semifinished products. The federal authorities have established fixed prices for a limited number of products and services such as sugar, electricity, tobacco, cigarettes, housing, transportation. Furthermore, local enterprises are obliged to report price increases to local authorities, but their freedom to change their prices according to

16 *Ibid.*, p. 254.
17 Kubović and Tričković, *op. cit.*, pp. 20–23.

changing supply-and-demand conditions is apparently seldom interfered with.

Some idea of the increasing independence of economic enterprises was provided by Janez Stanovnik when he compared the financial independence of American and Yugoslav enterprises:

[If] Jugoslav enterprises in 1959 [are] compared with American corporations over the period 1950–59 . . . [the results will show] that the American corporations paid 49.5 per cent of their gross profits in the form of direct taxation and the Yugoslav enterprises under comparable headings paid 56.3 per cent. Whereas the American corporations paid their owners 29.7 per cent of their gross profits in the form of dividends, the Yugoslav enterprises paid the community 13.7 per cent. Accordingly, the American corporations retained 20.8 per cent of their gross profits whereas the Yugoslav enterprises were left with 30 per cent at their disposal.[18]

Caution, however, should be exercised in taking Stanovnik's analysis at face value since American and Yugoslav corporations are not necessarily comparable.

Coordination of economic planning and the market is attempted in various ways. The foremost is that via investment policy. Though investments funds at the disposal of enterprises have grown considerably (from 57 per cent in 1959 to 63 per cent in 1960), the centralized funds of the federal government continue to play a strategic role. According to one estimate, one-third of the investment made from federal sources is sufficient to assure a balanced growth among all sectors of the economy as well as to encourage more rapid development of the country's backward areas, which constitute approximately one-third of Yugoslavia's area and population.[19] Furthermore, enterprises in the socialist as well as private sector take into consideration federal activities in the investment area in formulating their policies. As will be noted, however, many problems remain to be solved before the investment sector functions smoothly.

[18] Stanovnik, in *Foreign Affairs,* Jan. 1962, p. 259.
[19] *Ibid.,* p. 261.

Another way of influencing economic activity which is at the disposal of authorities is the turnover tax. Through it the authorities influence supply-and-demand conditions and so prices. This method is, however, becoming more important as a means of obtaining revenue than as a way of influencing economic activity, and even in the revenue field its importance is declining. In the Soviet Union, for example, between 1950 and 1959 the turnover tax represented 56.7 per cent of the total budgetary revenues, but in Yugoslavia in 1960 the tax represented only 19.3 per cent of the public revenues.[20]

Monetary and credit policies are growing means of influencing economic activity. Thus, in 1960, 33.2 per cent of the investments in fixed assets and 38.7 per cent of those in working capital were financed by bank loans, which in Yugoslavia is interpreted as a step in the direction of "more rational" utilization of resources.

THE YUGOSLAV SYNTHESIS AND ITS PROBLEMS

The problems arising out of the Yugoslav synthesis of planning and the market flow from two principal sources—at least as viewed by the Yugoslavs.[21] First, they derive from the underdeveloped character of the economy; second, from the incompleteness of the synthesis itself.

The economy still suffers from some of the drawbacks that characterize an underdeveloped economy. The low elasticities of supply and demand characteristic of underdeveloped economies, though less pronounced in Yugoslavia, plague the economy. The result is that the price system appears incapable, at least to Yugoslav authorities, of bringing about the structural changes that the authorities desire. As the economy continues to develop, there is hope, or so it is argued, that the higher elasticities which will result, especially in supply, will permit the price system to operate and so undertake the marginal and structural changes not dependent on external economies. One can share the hope of some

[20] *Ibid.*

[21] See, for example, the interesting discussion by Bora Jelić, "The Yugoslav Economic System," *Annals of Collective Economy,* 1958, pp. 116 ff.

Yugoslavs that the economy will be allowed to benefit from the broader application of the price system.

The second cause of the economy's problems is considered by Yugoslavs to be more serious. The country's rapid economic development and the apparent inability of the planning mentality to keep pace with changing developments have produced a number of serious problems. The first of these occurs in the field of international trade and concerns the appearance of severe distortions between domestic and foreign prices. A subsequent chapter will consider the country's trade problems in more detail. There is also the lack of a consistent pricing system, which makes it almost impossible to arrive at a rational system of prices. To this should be added the serious problem arising out of an inadequate system for marshaling investment resources and allocating them in the most efficient manner. A closer look at the banking system is also called for.

In addition to these problems, there are those arising out of the hitherto unsatisfactory attempts to reach a workable solution in the integration of economic activity among economic enterprises. This is particularly critical in such areas as research and development. The distribution of income within economic enterprises is also crying out for a satisfactory solution. It is insufficient merely to state that some people in an enterprise are making more money than others. This problem of wage differentials is particularly critical.

All of these difficulties, and indeed many others, are continually discussed in Yugoslav literature, though it is not always clear what effect, if any, such discussions have on policies. But then neglect of economic literature and professional advice, for better or worse, is something that Yugoslavia shares with other countries.

6.

WORKERS' MANAGEMENT

WORKERS' MANAGEMENT AND THE FIRM

The country's unique system of workers' management was put into effect with the passage of the Basic Law in the Management of Enterprises by the Working Collectives on June 27, 1950, by the People's Assembly of Yugoslavia.[1] The law transferred the operation and management of all factories and of all economic enterprises in general to the persons employed in such enterprises. The law, with its subsequent amendments, is based on the principle that, although an economic enterprise is public property, it is managed on behalf of the community by the firm's employees.

On the day that an economic enterprise is founded its employees are entitled to manage it. They elect their own workers' council and managing board from their own ranks on a nonremunerative basis. In enterprises with less than thirty employees the entire work force exercises the rights and obligations of the workers' council. The members of these two groups continue to work in their company jobs while serving their terms of office. A council may number from 15 to 120 members depending on the size and composition of the enterprise. The term of office of council members is one year, but they may be recalled within that period if they lose the confidence of their fellow employees. A council makes decisions pertaining to basic matters of economic activity,

[1] M. Bogosavljević and M. Pešaković, *Workers' Management of a Factory in Yugoslavia* (Belgrade: Jugoslavija Publishing House, 1959), p. 25.

organization, and internal relations in the establishment, determining the line of business policy which the managing board and director must pursue. It also supervises the managing board by passing on its reports and giving it instructions for future work. As its executive body a council elects a managing board for a term of one year subject to recall at any time within that period. A board consists of from 3 to 11 members, including the director of the enterprise. Its activities include (1) the preparation of proposals on matters under the exclusive jurisdiction of the workers' council; (2) elaboration and supervision of the enforcement of decisions and instructions of the workers' council; and (3) independent decisions on important current economic matters as well as on other matters falling within its jurisdiction by law or by the regulations of the enterprise itself.

Safety measures to prevent a managing board from becoming bureaucratic are set forth in provisions such as the requirement that three-fourths of a managing board must come from the ranks of workers directly engaged in production, that a new managing board may include no more than one-third of the members of the former managing board, and that no one may be elected to a managing board more than twice in succession. Members of a managing board are protected from falling under the undue influence of the director and other leading officers of the firm by the provision that they cannot be dismissed or transferred to another job without their own consent. A 1957 law regulating labor relations has extended such protection to the members of workers' councils. This law at the same time removed the members of these two groups from the area of disciplinary action by the enterprise by placing them under a special disciplinary council established by the competent municipal people's committee for all the enterprises within its territory.

With the passage of the Basic Law in 1950 the position of the director in the firm changed. No longer was he the sole management authority in a firm. Legally his position is that of top executive responsible for organizing the production in accord with the dictates of the workers' council and managing board and consistent with the laws and regulations pertaining to the organization and business of the enterprise.

We may illustrate the internal organization of an enterprise and its relations with the community by considering the Rade Končar Electrical Works in Zagreb.[2] The history of this enterprise started in 1925, when a Yugoslav branch of the German Siemens firm established a small electrical motor factory in Zagreb. Its purpose was to repair and assemble electrical motors with parts imported from Germany. Up to 1945 there was little expansion in the activity of the enterprise. In the decade following, however, the size and activities of the enterprise expanded considerably. In 1945 the enterprise had consisted of 4,302 square meters of factory space; by 1955, 68,000 square meters of factory space had been added. Total production of electric motors, transformers, and apparatus mounted consisted of 185 tons in 1946. By 1958 the volume of production had increased to over 9,000 tons. The number of employees in the period 1945–55 more than tripled.

Figure 2 illustrates the internal organization of the Rade Končar enterprise. At the top is the workers' council, whose rights and duties are determined by law and by the regulations of each enterprise. The regulations constitute the principal internal directive by which every enterprise conducts its affairs in the manner considered best suited to its particular conditions. The only proviso is that such regulations must be consistent with existing laws. They are approved by the municipal people's committee.

In the Rade Končar enterprise existing regulations allocate to the central workers' council the following functions:

1) Enactment of the enterprise's regulations and amendments, including the adoption of regulations dealing with labor relations, pay scales, and bonus system;
2) Adoption of the enterprise's annual financial statement;
3) Instruction of the managing board as to the activities to be carried out, as well as election and discussion of the board's members;

[2] *Ibid.*

THE RADE KONČAR ELECTRICAL WORKS WORKING COLLECTIVE, ZAGREB, YUGOSLAVIA, 1959

Central Workers' Council

- Managing Board
- General Manager
- Technical Committee

COMMISSIONS

- For Production and Organization
- For Financial and Economic Matters
- For Personnel Matters
- For Health and Safety
- For Social Standards
- For Requests and Complaints; Disciplinary Court

Department Workers' Councils

Dept. Workers' Council— Small Motors Production	Dept. Workers' Council— Med. Motors Production	Dept. Workers' Council— Large Motors Production	Dept. Workers' Council— Transformer Station Production	Dept. Workers' Council— Apparatus Production	Dept. Workers' Council— Tool Shop	Dept. Workers' Council— Auxiliary Plant	Dept. Workers' Council— Construction Office	Dept. Workers' Council— Technical Control	Dept. Workers' Council— Sales Sector	Dept. Workers' Council— Purchase Sector
COMMISSIONS	COMMISSIONS	COMMISSIONS	COMMISSIONS	COMMISSIONS	COMMISSIONS	COMMISSIONS	COMMISSIONS	COMMISSIONS	COMMISSIONS	COMMISSIONS
For Production and Organization	For Production and Organization	For Production and Organization	For Production and Organization	For Production and Organization	For Production and Organization	For Production and Organization				
For Financial and Economic Matters	For Financial and Economic Matters	For Financial and Economic Matters	For Financial and Economic Matters	For Financial and Economic Matters	For Financial and Economic Matters	For Financial and Economic Matters				
For Personnel Matters	For Personnel Matters	For Personnel Matters	For Personnel Matters	For Personnel Matters	For Personnel Matters	For Personnel Matters	For Personnel Matters	For Personnel Matters	For Personnel Matters	For Personnel Matters
For Health and Safety	For Health and Safety	For Health and Safety	For Health and Safety	For Health and Safety	For Health and Safety	For Health and Safety	For Economic Matters	For Economic Matters	For Economic Matters	For Economic Matters

4) Jurisdiction over matters concerning the fixed capital assets of the enterprise except in those cases where the amount is small in value, in which case the managing board or the director has jurisdiction;

5) The purchase and sale of patents and licenses; entrance into contracts for technical cooperation with other enterprises;

6) Loans for capital expenditures and operating funds;

7) The formation and application of the enterprise's reserve funds except in cases where this right has been transferred up to a specified amount to the managing board;

8) Distribution of that part of the enterprise's net profit that remains at the disposal of the enterprise;

9) Organization and disbanding of various departments and business units;

10) All decisions on affiliation with professional associations and election of the enterprise's representatives to the bodies of these associations and instruction of them in their work;

11) Adoption of a plan of training for employees and the granting of scholarships;

12) Naming of a disciplinary commission for purposes of conducting proceedings into breaches of labor discipline by all employees excluding the director and members of the workers' council and managing board.[3]

Under the Law on Labor Relations of 1957 the powers of the workers' councils in hiring and firing employees have been considerably expanded. The power to hire and fire employees, except for those on the managing staff, formerly rested with the director or the section managers and department heads. Since 1957 these powers have been vested in the council and its representative commission. The director of an enterprise notifies the commission regarding the quantity and qualifications of the required em-

[3] *Ibid.*, p. 31.

ployees or proposes dismissal of employees, but action is taken by the council's commission.

The managing board of the Rade Končar enterprise, consisting of eleven members including the director, is the executive body of the workers' council. According to law and its own regulations, it is empowered to draw up a draft of the basic production plan for the enterprise, a current operational plan, a proposal for the internal organization of the enterprise as well as job classifications, and proposals for business that fall within the competence of the workers' council; to appoint employees to posts of responsibility within the enterprise; and to make decisions involving appeals against the decisions of the director.[4]

The central workers' council of the Rade Končar enterprise has established seven standing commissions on its own initiative. These commissions are indicated in Figure 2. The establishment of such commissions by an enterprise is not obligatory. Indeed the Law on Labor Relations (1957) provides explicitly for only two standing commissions—one for discipline and the other for the hiring and firing of employees. In our example the duties of the latter commission are carried out by a commission for labor relations (the personnel commission). The difference between the commissions explicitly established by the 1957 law and those established on the initiative of the workers' council is that the former are authorized to decide in the final instance on matters within their jurisdiction whereas the latter are authorized merely to advise the workers' council. Only one other commission, the commission for social services, has certain powers specifically delegated to it.

Owing to the size of the Rade Končar enterprise and in the interests of efficiency, the central workers' council in 1955 established department workers' councils. They are, in effect, auxiliary organs of the central body. A number of other large enterprises throughout the country have adopted similar auxiliary bodies.

Although directors continue to play an important role in the

4 *Ibid.,* p. 36.

country's enterprises, the position appears to have been demoted with the establishment of the system of workers' management. The function now is that of carrying out the directions of the workers' council and managing board. The director does, however, have independent jurisdiction in some matters. He is authorized by law to represent the enterprise before the state authorities and in legal relations between other economic organizations and natural persons.

At the same time the director is a representative of the local community in which the enterprise is located. As such, he is obliged to see that all the decisions and actions of the workers' management bodies are within the framework and spirit of the law. He is empowered to set aside or hold up any decisions adopted by the workers' council or the managing board that he considers in violation of existing laws and the regulations of government authorities. The director's influence consequently is not insignificant. The council may, however, request his dismissal, as provided for under Article 96 of the Decree on the Founding of Enterprises and Shops.

There appear to be two connections between an enterprise and a community that are of primary importance. One is between the economic plans of the federal, republic, and communal levels of government and the production plan of the enterprise. The plan of the latter serves as a basis for federal, republic, and communal plans. At the same time these plans provide an enterprise with an over-all picture of the economic conditions within which it will operate.

The other important connecting link between the enterprise and the community is the various economic associations and chambers. These organizations can have a significant influence, for example, on the production plans and price policies of an enterprise.

Other important sources of influence on the activities of an enterprise are local organizations of the Trade Union Federation, the League of Communists, and the People's Youth Organization. According to law, the trade union in an enterprise is empowered to propose candidates to the workers' councils, to carry out decisions reached by the director, the workers' management, and other executive bodies, to propose dismissal of "inactive" or "irresponsible" members in any of the workers' management bodies, and to propose the convocation of the worker's council. Moreover, the trade union has considerable influence on the pay policy of the enterprise and on actions taken to ensure the health and safety of employees.

The role of the League of Communists in an enterprise is essentially political-educational in nature. Although the organization plays an important part in the distribution of the profits of an enterprise and in the personal income of employees, it does so jointly with the trade union and usually through the latter organization. Similarly, the People's Youth Organization within an enterprise devotes its main efforts to the professional training of the younger employees while at the same time preparing them for admission into the League of Communists.

WORKERS' MANAGEMENT IN PRACTICE

The operation of the system of workers' management has attracted considerable attention both within and without Yugoslavia. One writer comments on the system's operation from 1950 to 1955 as follows:

Yugoslav industrial workers are not in a position to control the policies of their firms either through the election procedures or through the agency of the workers' councils. . . . The preservation of the overall competence of the state, and the retention and in some cases the strengthening of the control organs . . . have left full power in the hands of the leaders of the state and party. But, despite this rather impressive array of constraints, the aims of the leaders were not fully realized . . . [and] some unwanted results were obtained.[5]

5 Benjamin Ward, "Workers' Management in Yugoslavia," *Journal of Political Economy*, Oct. 1957, pp. 379–80. Copyright 1957 by the University of Chicago and reprinted by permission of the publisher, the University of Chicago Press.

These "unwanted" results include increases in wages in industry and trade, less worker apathy, and a more serious attitude on the part of the worker-managers toward their responsibilities in hiring and firing directors. Such evidence in support of the importance of workers' councils is considered by some as weak. Benjamin Ward, for example, argues that the real centers of power rest with the director and managing board.[6] This should not be interpreted to mean that the actions of these organs are inconsistent with the desires of the other employees within an enterprise. Yet if we take the press reports and the speeches of the country's leaders seriously, the aims and desires of the director and managing board on the one hand and those of the employees on the other are frequently at cross purposes.

Branko Horvat and Vlado Raščović in commenting on Ward's study of the Yugoslav system of workers' management argue, in effect, that if the workers do not control the factories it makes little sense "to turn the whole economic organization upside down to make them behave as if they did."[7] Would it not be easier, they ask, to copy an already existing system, for example, the American or the Soviet?[8] Indeed, it probably would have been easier to copy either one of these systems since both have existed in the country— capitalism of a sort before World War II and the Soviet system after the war.

Such copying, however, would undoubtedly have led to undesirable political side effects—as these effects are interpreted by the Yugoslav leadership. For example, it would have been inconsistent with the Yugoslav view of workers' management as representing a higher level of political, social, and economic development than either the capitalist or Soviet systems. According to Horvat and Raščović, the Yugoslav system "came into existence as a reaction against the exploitation of workers in both the system of private ownership and in the economy run by the state bureaucracy. It

[6] *Ibid.*, p. 386.
[7] "Workers' Management in Yugoslavia: A Comment," *Journal of Political Economy*, Apr. 1959, p. 194.
[8] *Ibid.*

represents the realization of an old humanitarian and socialist ideal, and as such, it was met with general and genuine enthusiasm." [9]

The disagreement and confusion among supporters and critics of Yugoslavia's unique system of workers' management seem to me to be traceable to the implicit use of different criteria in judging the viability of the country's system. Critics appear to use as a criterion the ability of the system to give scope to "talent," such as directors and technicians. Supporters, on the other hand, use as their criterion the ability of the system to give scope to the "untalented," such as the production line workers. The "untalented" cannot translate their grievances into creative effort and so are likely to be more troublesome than the "talented." The problem then is how to give scope to the untalented while at the same time ensuring the system against them.

If judged by the latter criterion, the Yugoslav system appears well engineered. How well the system performs on this score is suggested by the success of so-called blue-collar workers (not all of whom are, of course, "untalented") in moving into managerial positions. In reviewing the operation of the system of workers' management from 1950 to 1960, Vladimir Farkaš reported that 76.5 per cent of the blue-collar workers and 23.5 per cent of the white-collar workers have participated in some capacity in managing the country's enterprises.[10] Over 70 per cent of these worker-managers had less than a United States high school education.

Examples provided by Horvat and Raščović will suffice to illustrate the type of problems against which the country has found it necessary to insure itself:

The views of the mass of unskilled workers—that, because everyone has the same needs, everyone has to get the same pay—have in a certain number of enterprises led to a leveling of wages and salaries. . . . The consequences were lack of responsibility, lack of initiative, lack of

---

[9] *Ibid.*, p. 197.
[10] "Uz deset godina radničkog samoupravljanja" ("Ten Years of Workers' Management"), *Ekonomski pregled* ("Economic Survey," Zagreb), no. 11–12 (1960), p. 802.

incentives, and, only after all this had become obvious, the radical correction of wage differentials in 1957. Similarly, there were tendencies to distribute all profits instead of investing them. . . . The administrative staff, to escape control or to preserve social prestige, tended to cast their reports in technical language incomprehensible to uneducated laymen.[11]

Some evidence of the degree to which "professionalization" of the managerial functions in a firm has occurred is available. Mirjana Poček in a study of 143 of the 193 enterprises located in the Zagreb area during the period 1953–58 concludes that "professionalization" does not seem to be a serious problem.[12] Her study is based on worker mobility into and out of offices in the principal organizations (president of the workers' council, president of the managing board, president of the trade union, and secretary of the League of Communists within an enterprise) . In order to compare the mobility in the various enterprises she constructs a mobility index M. The index measures the total number of people occupying the four principal offices during the six-year period of study. A large M indicates great mobility, with the theoretical size ranging from 4 to 24, i.e., 4×6, where $M = 4$ is minimum mobility and $M = 24$ maximum mobility. The results of her research indicate that M ranges from 6 to 20 and averages 12 in the 143 enterprises investigated, suggesting that the degree of mobility varies considerably among the enterprises. Unfortunately, we do not have a comparable study for the mobility of the director. Scattered evidence suggests, however, that his position is not as secure as the critics of the system would have one believe. On the other hand, it would be interesting to see how much the mobility of the key personnel depends on their political affiliations.

[11] *Op. cit.*, pp. 197–98.
[12] "Funkcionalna mobilnost u organima radničkog samoupravljanja" ("Functional Mobility in the System of Workers' Management") , *Ekonomski pregled,* no. 10 (1960) .

7.

THE FIRM

OBJECTIVES OF THE FIRM

The objectives of a firm are not always clear-cut. This is true for Yugoslavian firms as well as for those elsewhere. Simply asking a firm's managers what their objectives are does not necessarily yield satisfactory results. One soon discovers that managers agree to almost any plausible objective about which they are asked. Yugoslav worker-managers say that they wish to maximize their own incomes, maximize the firm's profits, maximize the firm's sales, minimize costs, and at the same time promote socialism. Since it is seldom possible to serve such a multiplicity of goals simultaneously, it is more important to determine what these managers do than what they say they do. Even the most casual observer will discover that they settle on one objective or some compromise among several.

In the private sector of the country's economy, which consists of small craftsmen, artisans, and farmers, the traditional conclusion that firms seek to maximize monetary profits seems applicable. This is simply another way of saying that in this sector a firm's decisions can be analyzed without recourse to a kind of budget restraint whose existence distinguishes the traditional analysis of the firm from that of the consumers. However, many of these firms may seek to maximize the owner's free time subject to the provision that his earnings exceed a certain minimum level. The existence of a heavy tax on the monetary earnings of private firms lends support to such behavior.

The directors of firms in the socialist sector may be interested in maximizing the firm's monetary profits because they are representatives of the local commune which receives a part of its income from a tax on the firm's profits. On the other hand, these directors may be interested in maximizing the firm's total revenue or the money value of its sales, subject to a provision that profits should not fall below a certain acceptable level. As long as profits do not fall below such a level, the directors may devote a considerable amount of energy to expanding the firm's sales. The pursuit of such a goal can be rationalized on the ground that the directors of socialist firms wish not only to maintain their firms' competitive positions, which are partly dependent on the size of the enterprise, but to overwhelm competitive firms in the private sector and so promote socialism.

Such behavior would depend on the "socialist consciousness" of the director and other worker-managers as well as on what is perhaps a more important issue—whether their salaries are related to the size of the firm's operations or to its profits.[1] By and large, the bulk of the worker-managers in Yugoslav socialist firms are interested in the pedestrian goal of maximizing their individual incomes. And since 1950 their incomes have depended in part on the firm's profits. Unfortunately, such attitudes on the part of the worker-managers may impose severe restrictions on the operations of the Yugoslav firm.

THE FIRM'S REVENUE, COSTS, AND PROFITS

Although the government reserves the right to intervene in the affairs of Yugoslav firms, the firm is responsible for the production and sale of its products. The worker-managers in these firms are free to set price and output policy according to their own material interests. The criterion for a firm's successful operation is its

[1] For a discussion of the relations between firm size and salaries of executives, see Marshall R. Colberg *et al.*, *Business Economics* (Homewood, Ill.: Richard D. Irwin, 1957), pp. 376–79.

ability to earn revenue (in the usual meaning of the word) to cover cost. Costs do not have the same meaning as they do in Western countries because of the peculiarities in the wage system and social ownership of the means of production.

The definition and control of costs have been particularly vexing to the Yugoslavs. Since 1952, when many of the Soviet type of controls were abolished, a particular type of financial control has developed which has gradually come to embrace all managers of social property. In the beginning it was called "social evidence" and was limited to industrial enterprises. It has subsequently grown into a widespread system of "social-bookkeeping" with the passage of the Law of Social Bookkeeping on October 16, 1959. The responsibility for this financial surveillance is with the National Bank. The transfer of deposit accounts serves as the basis for this surveillance.

As defined by law, labor costs are based on the average skill of workers in the industry. For these purposes firms are divided into several groups and labor costs per worker per month are established for each group.[2] For example, if a firm falls into an industry group for which wages per worker are established at, say, 10,000 dinars per month and the firm has a complement of 10 people, then its wage cost for the month is 10 times 10,000 or 100,000 dinars. These 10,000 dinars per month represent the "calculated" wage, which is not the same thing as the "contractual" wage that the firm is free to set and that is the basis for hiring the firm's staff. The calculated wage set by the government serves as an accounting cost to the firm. The calculated wage computed as a percentage of the contractual wage at planned levels of output and prices is lower than the contractual wage. But in order for a worker to receive his contractual wage the firm must make a profit. And this is no guarantee that the individual worker will receive his share of the profits since a share goes first to various reserve funds and the local government. What remains is at the disposal of the workers'

---

[2] See the various issues of *Ekonomika preduzeća* ("Business Economics," Belgrade) since 1957 and Benjamin Ward, "The Firm in Illyria: Market Syndicalism," *American Economic Review*, Sept. 1958, pp. 566–89.

council, which may reinvest these profits rather than pay a sort of "worker dividend."

Other costs incurred by the firm such as for the use of land and capital equipment are also set by the government and serve as important regulatory devices. The firm is required to pay rent for the use of land equal to the rate paid on the largest class of arable land in the district. Computed on a cadastral basis, the rate is in accordance with the yield of the land in question. Charges for the use of capital equipment by the firm and the depreciation rates for such equipment are set by the authorities and apparently discriminate among various industries for the purpose of inducing fulfillment of the country's annual economic plans.

Thus costs to the Yugoslav firm are the sum of the calculated wage fund, interest on short-term borrowing, interest on fixed assets, rent on land, material costs, and the various taxes levied by the government.[3] The difference between a firm's costs thus defined and revenue are its "profits."

INCOME-MAXIMIZING WORKER-MANAGERS

For purposes of analysis let us accept *in toto* the argument that worker-managers in Yugoslav firms manage and operate the country's socialized enterprises in their own material interests. We assume that these interests are best served by maximizing the individual incomes of worker-managers. What are the implications of such a system and such behavior for the firm? A useful way of gaining some insight into these implications is by considering the problem of factor allocation. For this purpose I shall draw on Benjamin Ward's study of an Illyrian firm. When a number of modifications are made on Ward's firm, the Yugoslav socialist firm is very closely approximated.

Let us assume that the Yugoslav socialist firm and a firm in the private sector, which we shall call a "capitalist firm," have identical production functions and that they are operating under identical market conditions. Consider now the case of a firm with two

---

[3] Ward, *op. cit.*, p. 568.

variable inputs (*Z* and *L*) producing a single output *G*. In Figure 3 the quantities of the two factors of production *Z* and *L*, where *Z*

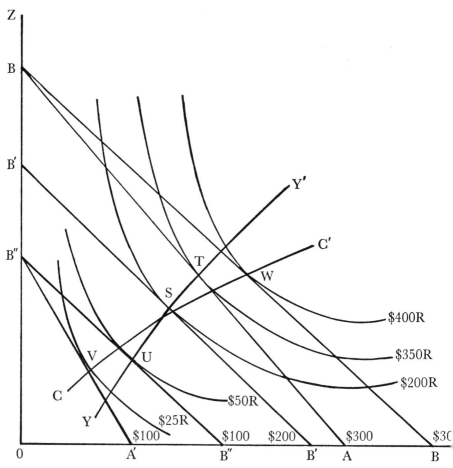

Figure 3. Yugoslav capitalist and socialist firms. For an explanation of the figure, see the text.

represents capital or some other factor and *L* represents labor, are measured along the two axes. The production indifference curves, usually called isoquants (equal quantities), show the different combinations of the two factors which can produce given quantities of the finished product *G*. By multiplication of these quantities by a given constant price for product G an isorevenue curve can be obtained which is identical to the isoquant curve. In effect, the isorevenue curves are nothing more than isoquants measured in terms of dollars. For example, the isorevenue curve labeled $400R shows all the combinations of the two factors Z and L which will produce $400 of revenue; the isorevenue $350R shows the different quantities of the two factors which will produce $350 of revenue; and so forth. The isorevenue curves are drawn convex to the origin because the underlying isoquant curve is so drawn to indicate that the two factors are not perfect substitutes for each other and that the more of one factor that is used relative to the other, the more difficult it becomes to substitute yet further quantities of it for the other factor.

The lines BB, BA, B'B', B"B", and B"A' represent equal outlay or isocost. A fundamental theorem of rational behavior is that an increase in the price of L would reduce the amount of L employed with a given outlay; less L would be employed with the outlay line BA, BB, and so forth. To achieve a firm's aim of maximizing profit, the firm must go to a point of tangency between an isorevenue and isocost because it is at such points that a given isocost comes in contact with the highest isorevenue, i.e., maximum output at given cost, and a given isorevenue comes in contact with the lowest isocost, i.e., given output at minimum cost. The curves YY' and CC' or expansion paths are the locus of all such points of tangency for the Yugoslav firm (YY') and for the capitalist firm (CC'). For given relative prices of the two inputs (the slope of the isocost line), the expansion path tells us how the firm's optimum input combination will vary when the size of its input budget or isocost line changes.

Consider first the capitalist firm's equilibrium point W in Figure 3. At this point the capitalist firm is producing $400R worth of revenue with a factor input mix determined by the relative prices of factors L and Z and represented by the slope of the line BB. At this point it is making a "profit" because its isorevenue ($400R) exceeds its isocost ($300). But W is not an equilibrium position for the Yugoslav socialist firm because line

BB is not the Yugoslav firm's relevant isocost line. It is instead the isocost line *BA*, whose slope is steeper indicating a higher relative price for factor *L*. The steeper slope for line *BA* is due to the fact that one must take into account the profit shares of worker-managers, and this results in a higher price for labor inputs. Consequently, the Yugoslav firm is in equilibrium at point *T* on a lower isorevenue producing $350R of revenue with the same outlay ($300) as the capitalist firm but employing less labor than the capitalist firm.

If now the price of product *G* falls to a zero profit point, say to *S*, where the isorevenue curve $200R is equal to isocost line $200, the capitalist firm contracts its operations along curve *CC'* and the Yugoslav socialist firm contracts along *YY'*. The two firms will meet at point *S* because at this point profits to each firm are zero. There is nothing for the worker-managers to share and thereby raise the price of the labor input. The isocost line *B'B'* is relevant for both firms. At the zero point *S* each firm is producing a revenue of $200 with a total outlay for each firm of $200. Thus, the Yugoslav firm and capitalist firm produce identical outputs and employ the same factor input mix when profits are zero. These results contain important implications for long-run analysis, which we shall discuss.

Should the price of product *G* drop even more so that both firms are incurring losses, then according to Figure 3 the Yugoslav firm will contract to point *U* and the capitalist firm to point *V*. With identical outlays of $100 the Yugoslav firm is now producing $50R revenue while the capitalist firm is producing $25R of revenue and using less labor than the Yugoslav firm. This is so because the worker-managers are now interested in spreading the losses among as many workers as possible. The empirical relevance of such a situation is limited. In the first place, the authorities guarantee a minimum wage to each worker-manager based on a percentage of the calculated wage. In the second place, the Yugoslav system provides for bankruptcy if a firm cannot meet its regular financial obligations to its staff and government.[4]

---

[4] *Ibid.*, pp. 566–89.

Simple and abstract though our model and analysis are, they contain the essence of many of the difficulties in the country's economy. The push and pull between the country's local commune responsible for the economic activity within its territory and the worker-managers of firms within its territory is but a case in point. Since the commune receives a percentage of a firm's total profit as part of its income, it is interested in seeing to it that a firm maximizes total profits. Moreover, it has considerable interest in maintaining maximum employment within its area and especially in industry. In addition to the obvious economic consideration, there is also the political consideration and Communist penchant for creating as many industrial workers as possible because of their political reliability. All of these goals appear to be in collision with those of the worker-management.

President Tito's speech in Split in May 1962 aptly summarized the official complaints usually leveled against the income-maximizing worker-managers.[5] Such practices as raising prices without regard to underlying market conditions, using funds earmarked for investment to raise wages, firing workers who raised their voices in criticism, and unfair competition in dealings abroad by domestic enterprises were selected for particular criticism. Even sharper criticism was directed at enterprises that were formed to conduct foreign trade but whose only export product appeared to have been the globe-trotting members of the enterprise.

In November 1961 Tito delivered a similar speech in Skoplje.[6] He criticized the insufficient attention paid to economic factors in establishing new industrial capacity. In order to obtain means for economic development, each republic, district, and commune desires to establish industrial enterprises, often unnecessarily duplicating facilities existing elsewhere. Such proliferation of production, Tito argued, robs the country of the economies of scale that could be realized by a greater concentration of production facilities. And again he reserved his sharpest criticism for those enterprises and their workers' management councils that had recently

[5] *Politika* (Belgrade), May 7, 1962.
[6] *Ibid.*, Nov. 14, 1961.

raised their prices for the purpose of increasing their funds to raise the wages of their employees.

Unfortunately such criticism is usually ineffective because it asks the worker-managers to behave in a way that is contrary to their economic interests. Unless backed by something more than appeals, such criticism tends to fall on deaf ears. And indeed the authorities do have at their disposal means more effective than words with which to impress their wishes on the worker-managers in particular and on the economy in general. These means do not include adoption of directives of the market socialist economy of the Lange-Lerner type. One very good reason for the inapplicability of such directives in Yugoslavia is indicated by the case of a firm whose worker-managers are asked to act in a way that does not exactly coincide with their motivations. Theoretically at least, the Yugoslav system is superior to the other type in that it avoids the pitfalls of marginal cost pricing inherent in Lange's "socialism by price guidance." Lange's method of pricing dictates that every firm sell as much as it produces and at a price equal to marginal cost. But what happens in the case of a firm whose average costs decrease as its production increases? According to the standard average marginal relations, when average costs are falling, marginal cost is less than average cost. Consequently, if the firm sells at a unit price equal to marginal cost, the price must be less than average cost. In effect, unit costs exceed unit returns and the firm loses money on each and every unit it sells. What is more, the managers of such a firm, no matter how efficient they are, can do nothing to make any profit so long as they stick to the rule of a marginal cost price. Since they share in a firm's profits, this would hardly be a satisfactory solution to them.

By altering the relative prices of factor inputs the authorities can influence the operation of the Yugoslav socialist firm. If the authorities desire to push such a firm toward the capitalist firm's equilibrium point W, they can do so by increasing the relative price of the other factor Z (Figure 3). Such an increase will move the BA line closer to the capitalist firm's isocost line BB. The Yugoslav firm will then be induced to increase its output and use more labor.

If the other factor Z is, say, capital, the authorities can induce the worker-managers to push their firm's operation toward point W by increasing the price or interest rate at which the firm can obtain capital funds. This helps to explain, for example, why the Yugoslav authorities for all practical purposes dropped a system of investment auctions soon after it was instituted. Rather than bid for investment funds and, *ceteris paribus,* increase the price of such funds, it is to the interest of worker-managers to keep the price as low as possible.

Instead of capital we may let Z represent raw material inputs to the firm. The authorities may induce the firm to operate in the desired direction by changing the prices of the inputs. As a matter of fact the price of some raw material is controlled by the authorities, though the reason ususally given is that such control helps to eliminate monopoly.

Moreover, the authorities can and do directly affect the incomes of worker-managers with a progressive profits tax on the firm. Such a tax can also be coupled with a reduction in the calculated wage rate, thereby increasing the effectiveness of the tax in inducing worker-managers to operate in a desired fashion.

But the difficulty with all these means is that they encourage intervention in the economy. This is the very thing that the Yugoslavs have attempted to discourage since 1952. Intervention in one area of the economy leads to intervention in other areas. As the Yugoslavs know from experience, when controls and directives multiply it is at the expense of the economy. Moreover, intervention uses scarce resources, especially "human capital," which tends to be in seriously short supply in an underdeveloped country like Yugoslavia.

Let us assume that Yugoslavia produces two goods, X produced by firms in the socialist sector of the economy and Y by firms in the private sector.[7] The quantity of X may be measured along a horizontal axis and that of Y along a vertical. Let us also suppose that Yugoslavia is a country of many identical individuals and that

---

[7] The following analysis is adapted from Milton Friedman, "The 'Welfare' Effects of an Income Tax and an Excise Tax," *Essays in Positive Economics* (Chicago: University of Chicago Press, 1953), pp. 106–11.

tastes, preferences, and the kind and quantity of resources at the disposal of each individual are identical. In a hypothetical Yugoslavia so constituted, every individual will have the same income and consume the same bundle of goods. Consequently we can represent the position of any one individual's indifference curves as GG', and HH', in Figure 4. With the resources available to the

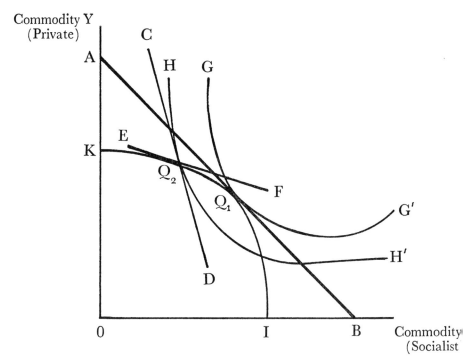

Figure 4. The private and the socialist sectors. For an explanation of the figure, see the text.

country it is technically possible to produce some set of combinations of X and Y. These combinations can be represented by a production indifference curve such as KI in Figure 4. AB represents the consumer's budget line.

In full competitive equilibrium for our hypothetical Yugoslavia, each individual would be at Q_1. His rate of substitution in consumption as represented by the slope of the consumption indifference curve GG' would be equal to the rate of substitution in purchase in the market as represented by the price ratio indicated by the slope of the budget line AB, which is equal to the rate of substitution in production represented by the slope of the production indifference curve KI. Since Q_1 is on the frontier of the production indifference curve, all of the technical possibilities are being fully utilized.

Consider the wedge driven by worker-managers between the price of X relevant to producers and the price relevant to consumers. For all practical purposes the wedge is an excise tax levied by worker-managers on the price of the product X in the sense that their operations are a deviation from full competitive conditions. As such, the position of equilibrium is given by Q_2, which satisfies the conditions that a constant-receipts line (EF) be tangent to the production indifference curve and that the consumer budget line (CD) be tangent to a consumption indifference curve. The angle between the two lines EF and CD is the excise tax on X levied by the worker-managers producing X in the socialist sector because they act as if the net price to them were lower than it is. If the initial position was one of full competitive equilibrium, the position Q_2 is inferior because the individual is on a lower indifference curve HH'.

One way to eliminate the divergence caused by profit sharing by the worker-managers is for the authorities to impose an excise tax on product Y produced by the private sector equal in percentage to the tax imposed on X by the worker-managers. Such an excise tax would eliminate the divergence between the price ratio relevant to consumers and that relevant to producers, and thus the position would shift from Q_2 to Q_1. With an excise tax on Y the equilibrium position starting from a position Q_2 is now Q_1. Although there is little reason to believe that the authorities do in fact have such an analysis or objective in mind, it does help to explain why the private sector of the economy has been the object of continuing economic discrimination in the form of various taxes that could be loosely labeled "excise taxes."

To judge from Figure 3, at the zero profit point the Yugoslav socialist firm and the capitalist firm are identical. This suggests that in the long run the two firms might achieve identical positions regarding output and employment. Unlike the situation in capitalist countries, however, the entry of new socialist firms takes a different path in Yugoslavia. By and large, new firms, as already discussed, are organized at the initiative of local heads of government, though private individuals and existing firms play important roles in their inception and organization.

The importance of the economic long run in mitigating some of the less desirable features in the Yugoslav system can be further illustrated with the aid of Figure 4. The production indifference curve in the long run will tend to have less of a curvature than in the short run. The effect is to reduce and perhaps even eliminate the wedge between the price ratio relevant to producers in the socialist sector and the price ratio relevant to consumers. But, unfortunately, long-run positions are constantly changed by shifts in demand, imports, costs, and so forth, and the nonoptimal nature of the short-run solution under a worker-management system suggests a rather chronic lack of full efficiency compared with the competitive capitalist firm.

CONCLUSION

The outstanding feature of the Yugoslav socialist firm is the role played by worker-managers. This role differentiates the socialist firm from its capitalist counterpart in such matters as employment and output. As a consequence there is a departure from optimum conditions of received theory—at least in the short run.

This does not mean that the Yugoslav system is not workable. It does mean that it is not fully efficient in the economic sense. Unlike the profit-maximizing capitalist firm in received theory, the decision rule to maximize the individual incomes of worker-managers imposes on the Yugoslav socialist firm a sort of budget restraint which is analogous to that of the consumer in traditional theory. As long as socialist firms "spend" no more than the maximum profit which they could have earned under the traditional decision rule, the Yugoslav system can survive.[8] Yugoslav literature has recently devoted considerable attention to the idea that a worker should be paid according to his productivity.[9] It is not clear from these discussions whether the existing system would be modified in some way so as to increase its efficiency. Moreover, it is difficult to determine the precise meaning attached to productivity in these discussions. If payment according to productivity is taken to mean some sort of payment on a piece-rate basis, how then is such a criterion to be applied to the various service industries, say, for example, medicine and education?

Theoretically the system can be made to operate efficiently, but at the cost of a considerable amount of intervention. And such intervention is no guarantee that desirable results will in fact be produced. One suggestion for improving the system is to broaden the profit-sharing base. For example, instead of worker-managers sharing in the profits of their firm, the profits of the various firms could be pooled by the commune and then shared in a periodic dividend by all worker-managers within the commune's territory. The worker-managers would then have an incentive to adopt the traditional decision rule and maximize the firm's profits. But such a solution might very well result in a misallocation of resources among the country's communes.

[8] For a more detailed analysis of various nontraditional decision rules, see Gary S. Becker, "Irrational Behavior and Economic Theory," *Journal of Political Economy*, Feb. 1962, pp. 1–13.

[9] See, for example, Mika Špiljak, "Results, Problems and Tasks in the Field of Internal Relationships in Workers' Collectives," *Ekonomika preduzeća*, Nov. 1962, pp. 723–28. For an analysis of surplus labor in Yugoslav socialist firms, see Ward's discussion (*op. cit.*, pp. 584–85) of the phenomenon known as the "dead brigades" (*mrtve brigade*). His conclusion suggests that no contradiction exists between a firm's desire to emphasize capital inputs rather than labor inputs and its wish at certain times to give the appearance that surplus labor exists in its organization. The "in group" will "tolerate surplus labor" in the firm as long as such labor does not share in the profits and is paid below the calculated wage. This is one method, according to Ward, for reducing "accounting profits and hence the amount of taxation under the steeply progressive profits tax."

Although the Yugoslav system has its shortcomings, it is a marked improvement over the pre-1952 period of central planning. The new system has undoubtedly increased the efficiency of labor by its improvement of the incentive system. And after all, our illustrative figures are drawn on the basis of efficient use of the various factors of production.

8.

THE BANKING SYSTEM

CHARACTERISTICS OF THE BANKING SYSTEM

The banking system in Yugoslavia is undergoing constant change to meet the requirements of the rapidly changing economy. When the country began to decentralize economic activity, significant changes also occurred in the banking system.[1] By 1959 its system was of the multibank type consisting of a National Bank (central bank), an Investment Bank, a Foreign Trade Bank, an Agricultural Bank, communal or municipal banks, and cooperative and city savings organizations. As indicated in Table 11, 727 banks of various types and their branches operated in the country at the end of 1959.

The National Bank regulates the total stock of money and the volume of credit, provides for uniform domestic and foreign payment transactions, gathers economic intelligence, and since 1959 has been responsible for maintaining financial surveillance over the economy, with changes in deposit accounts serving as a basis for such surveillance. The Investment Bank administers the resources of the country's General Investment Fund as well as those of the several republics for the purpose of granting both

---

[1] D. Dimitrijević, "The Financial System of the Yugoslav Economy" (MS, 1961); Branko Mijović, "Kreditno-monetarni sistem" ("Credit and Monetary System"), in *Privredni sistem i ekonomska politika* ("Economic System and Economic Policy"); Belgrade: Rad, 1961), pp. 91–118; Miloš Vučković, "The Recent Development of the Money and Banking System of Yugoslavia," *Journal of Political Economy,* Aug. 1963, pp. 363–77.

TABLE 11. Number of banks and branches by types at ends of years, 1959–62

Type of Bank	1959	1960	1961	1962
Communal banks	380	375	380	356
Cooperative savings banks	177	179	—	—
Yugoslav Bank for Foreign Trade	12	12	10	10
Federal Investment Bank	30	30	27	9
Yugoslav Agricultural Bank	9	9	10	10
Municipal savings banks	9	9	6	—
National Bank	110	116	439	448 *
Total	727	730	872	833

Source: National Bank of Yugoslavia, *Annual Report 1959* (Belgrade: The Bank, 1960), p. 59. The figures for 1961–62 are from the Research Department of the Bank.
* Of this number 7 are branches of the National Bank and 441 are conducting "social" bookkeeping.

short-term and long-term loans for economic development. Influence over the country's foreign trade is exercised by the Foreign Trade Bank in its role of extending loans and acting as domestic intermediary for enterprises engaged in external trade. The Agricultural Bank is concerned primarily with the affairs of the agricultural sector. It extends, and supervises the use of, credit in agricultural and irrigation projects, carries out the government's agricultural subsidy programs, and employs credits made available to the country from abroad for agricultural purposes. Local financing of economic activity is undertaken by communal banks. These banks finance enterprises engaged in such activities as retail trade, handicrafts, tourist facilities, and other activities of a strictly local nature including participation in the consumer loan market. Cooperative savings organizations perform banking operations for their members and extend loans to farmers' cooperatives and farm enterprises of small and medium size. The city savings organizations deal mainly with the savings of local residents and provide funds for the construction and repair of dwellings and for farm and consumer financing. These cooperative savings organizations and the city savings organizations were abandoned in 1961 and their functions, for the most part, allocated to communal banks.

CHANGES IN THE BANKING AND CREDIT SYSTEM

In order to obtain a proper perspective on the country's banking and credit system and the numerous changes that have taken place, it is necessary to examine the peculiar position of banking in the country. Unlike the fractional reserve commercial banking system common in other parts of the world, banks in Yugoslavia cannot on their own initiative determine the volume of credit and deposits. The quantity of new credit is determined annually by the yearly Federal Social Plan. Moreover, the Federal Executive Council is empowered to activate or neutralize components of the money supply as a way of controlling deflationary or inflationary pressures.

Although bank notes and other hand-to-hand currency are the dominant means for carrying out internal payments for households and for firms outside the social sector, economic enterprises and all other organizations within the socialist sector are required by law to carry out their payments by the transfer of balances in bank deposit accounts. These deposit accounts serve the fourfold purpose of transferring payments, mobilizing "free" money, disposing of bank credits, and providing the means whereby banks can exercise financial control over depositors. At the same time such a system of transfer disposes of the necessity for clearinghouses since checks are not used to any significant degree.

With decentralization and the appearance of a more flexible economic system, the Soviet type of central credit planning was found to be inconsistent with the new system and so abandoned. Previously every economic enterprise had been entitled to the amount of bank credit allocated to it by the economic plan. Under the new system the quantity of bank credit extended to an enterprise is based on its financial soundness. The enterprise is now required to meet certain minimum qualifications, and among the most important is its ability to earn income. Failure to meet these qualifications does not necessarily prevent it from obtaining credit. It may obtain credit provided some political unit on the local, republic, or federal level guarantees that the debt will be repaid.

Before 1952 interest charged on loans served mainly to cover a bank's overhead expenses. Indeed, many loans were granted to enterprises without any interest charges. The movement of funds within an enterprise was planned. Recent changes have placed more importance on the role of interest rates as a means of allocating funds among competitors for funds. And as noted in Chapter 7, variations in interest rates are a potent means available to the authorities for influencing worker-managers to behave in a desired way. The rates actually charged, however, are established by the social plan and differ according to the type of credit, region, branch of economic activity, and sector of the economy. They range from 1 to 2 per cent in the favored areas of the socialist sector of the economy to 7 per cent for private producers. Depositors, on the other hand, earn 5 per cent on deposits.

Banks now have authority to increase their activity in the field of consumer loans. Previously consumer credit was extended only if an individual demonstrated some dire financial emergency. The total amount of such credit never exceeded one billion dinars. Consumer credit is now extended to any employed person up to a fixed percentage of his income and can be used to purchase all sorts of durable goods including automobiles. At the end of 1961 the amount of consumer credit outstanding was 142.5 billion dinars.

One of the most important roles that the banking system plays in the country's economy is that of financial surveillance over economic activity in the socialist sector. The National Bank is responsible for such surveillance and is assisted in this task by the other banks. The decentralization of the economic system with maintenance of an important role for economic planning at the same time has forced the Yugoslavs into a sort of bookkeeping arrangement involving the bulk of the economy. Since the Law of Social Bookkeeping was enacted only at the end of 1959, it is still too early to judge its effects. The administrative and paper work must, however, be substantial. Such a system of national book-keeping may reintroduce economic controls through the back door.

Since March 1961 and the enactment of new banking legislation the country has taken another important step in increasing the ability of the banking system to deal more adequately with the country's system of worker-management. Hitherto banks were not empowered to discount trade bills, and interenterprise financing of trade was expressly forbidden. The Yugoslav banking system has now adopted a technique for granting short-term credit to economic enterprises that is a wide departure from previous practice but one that is familiar to commercial banking practice elsewhere in the world. This is the technique of discounting short-term commercial bills.[2]

Though still in its formative stage, the technique appears to be an extension of the "real bill's doctrine" to the output of the country's socialist enterprises. It is envisioned to serve the needs of trade by providing an "appropriately elastic supply of money." Unfortunately this is not the result, as the sad experience of a few countries who adopted the doctrine will testify. Any definition of a "real bill" will of necessity be arbitrary. And the concept of reflux implicit in the doctrine is notoriously wobbly.

The chances are, however, that the Yugoslavs will not go so far as to adopt the "real bill's doctrine" in toto. But to the extent that they do adopt it, or indeed any of its elements however minor, provision should be made to handle the less desirable side effects that such an application will have on the money supply and the economy. According to the Yugoslav view, provision has already been made to handle the less desirable side effects.

AN APPRAISAL OF THE BANKING SYSTEM

The country's banking system is unlike that of any other country. This is particularly true since 1961, when the banking system was brought more in line with the country's novel system of

[2] Dragoljub Velizarić, "Menični eskon kao oblik kreditiranja" ("Discount Rate as a Form of Crediting"), *Ekonomika preduzeća* ("Business Economics"), Dec. 1962, pp. 807–12.

worker-management. Banks now have workers' councils that are at least theoretically similar to those in other branches of the economy.[3] Aside from the activities of a country's central bank, banking in most other parts of the world is conducted in the hope of earning a profit. It is a business, and bankers are for the most part businessmen. They seek profits through banking and investing. The funds of a bank are obtained in part from the bank's own capital. But by far the most important sources of funds are deposits.

All this is very different in the Yugoslav banking system. The worker-managers in the country's banks are not equivalent to bankers, as that occupation is usually understood, in Western countries. Indeed, they are not very much like the worker-managers in other branches of the country's economy since the latter have some voice in their firm's input, output, and price policies. Banking and other businesses are sharply differentiated in Yugoslavia.

The upper management group in Yugoslav banks is appointed directly by authorities at the various levels of government. Thus even the National Bank has its worker-managers, but they do not appreciably influence the Bank's policies. The governor and vice-governors of the Bank are appointed directly by the Federal Executive Council. The Bank's earnings consist of commission charges together with a portion of its receipts as fixed yearly by the Federal Executive Council. The worker-managers concern themselves with the more pedestrian tasks of handling various executive duties, including the labor relations of its own staff. This suggests that for all practical purposes the National Bank is, in effect, the financial arm of the Federal Executive Council. Little effort is made to maintain the fiction so prevalent in other countries that the central bank is independent of the central government.

[3] See Tihomir Stanojević, "Uloga i razvoj bankarskog sistema FNRJ" ("The Role and Development of Banking System in FDRY"), *Glasnik narodne banke* ("Bulletin of National Bank"), no. 6 (1962), pp. 3–16, and R. P. (only initials of authors are given in the section devoted to comments), "Prva godina rada saveta kolektiva narodne banke FNRJ," *ibid.*, no. 7 (1962), pp. 25–31.

The country's specialized banks such as the Investment Bank, the Foreign Trade Bank, and the Agricultural Bank have workers' councils, but as with the National Bank the upper management group is appointed by the Federal Executive Council. The resources at their disposal are obtained from the National Bank, foreign credits, and long-term deposits. These banks extend credit through the communal banks and lend directly only as prescribed in the Federal Social Plan. Extension of foreign credits must first be approved by the Federal Executive Council.

Communal banks are perhaps the nearest thing in the country to commercial banks in the sense that they are in direct contact with every economic and noneconomic enterprise within their territories. Unlike commercial banks, however, the liabilities of a communal bank are guaranteed by the entire commune's economy. Its board of directors consists of representatives from the commune's various economic and social organizations. A board's members are required to hold public meetings with their clients for the purpose of reviewing economic conditions and establishing the quantity of credit that the bank will extend in a subsequent period. Communal banks are required to send their balance sheets to every customer at least thirty days before the annual meeting. A commune's entire free resources are deposited with the communal bank, and it acts as banker to the entire commune. When authorized by the National Bank, these communal banks may carry out foreign exchange transactions, exercise insurance functions, and conduct lotteries as well as perform post-office duties.[4]

Some indication of the extent to which decentralization has occurred is provided by the fact that there has been a substantial transfer of assets and liabilities from the National Bank to other banks. This is indicated by the evidence summarized in Table 12.

Even more important from the viewpoint of decentralization has been the emergence of communal banks in the credit field. Thus the total volume of short-term credits of communal banks increased from 531 billion dinars in 1959 to 1,369 billion dinars in

4 Vučković, op. cit., p. 376.

TABLE 12. Distribution of credits and monetary resources by individual banks at ends of years, 1957–62 (*in billions of dinars*)

Year	National Bank		Other banks	
	CREDITS	DEPOSITS	CREDITS	DEPOSITS
1957	693	577	530	529
1958	679	551	650	661
1959	798	628	756	763
1960	960	768	864	878
1961	453	230	1615	1638
1962	560	362	1920	1920

Source: Research Department, National Bank of Yugoslavia.

1961. During the same period the short-term credits of the National Bank decreased from 798 billion dinars to 451 billion dinars. This does not mean that the influence of the National Bank is insignificant. Indeed, in 1961 about half of the liabilities of communal banks were to the National Bank. Some idea of the growing importance of communal banks is provided in Table 13.

TABLE 13. Consolidated balance sheet of communal banks, 1959, 1961, and 1962 (*in billions of dinars*)

	1959	1961	1962
Short-term credits of enterprises	424	1,175	1,362
Short-term credits to government organs	12	10	17
Long-term credits to economy	18	31	41
Consumer credits	70	128	169
Time deposits	137	155	297
Demand deposits	227	526	850
Debts to other banks	353	970	964

Source: Miloš Vučković, "The Recent Development of the Money and Banking System of Yugoslavia," *Journal of Political Economy*, Aug. 1963, p. 376. The 1962 estimates are from the Research Department, National Bank of Yugoslavia.

It is not too difficult to understand the hesitancy about turning over the banking system to banker worker-managers. Banking occupies a unique position in modern economies. The technical nature of modern production makes production in anticipation of demand unavoidable; and since the banking system is the agency supplying the funds which make this possible, the continuance of modern productive processes depends upon the functioning of the banking system. In effect, the banking system by its power to grant or withhold credit controls the very lifeblood of every large-scale productive activity. It would be indeed difficult for Yugoslavia's leaders to carry out their current type of economic planning without an adequate and assured source of commercial credit for their use. If the banking system were controlled by banker worker-managers, they could, by restricting the supplies of credit, make the execution of the Social Plan even more difficult than it is already. This is a risk that the current leadership is not very likely to take.

That the danger is not baseless the discussion in Chapter 7 makes plain. Worker-managers in a firm acting in their own material interests may very well restrict output. It is conceivable that the banker worker-managers might behave similarly and restrict the "output" of their firm, which is of course bank credit. Such a restriction might slow down capital accumulation and so have serious consequences for the country's economy. Bank credit tends to free investors from the voluntary abstinence routine of savers as well as relieve the authorities from more direct intervention in the economy as a means of raising the required savings. "Forced savings" via bank credit are an important means of capital accumulation. There are, however, definite limits to the amount of capital accumulation that can be acquired by this inflationary method.

It is not altogether speculation to argue that the representatives of socialist firms on the board of directors of a communal bank tend to take a more liberal attitude than the banker worker-managers toward interest rates and the quantity of credit that a bank extends. The banker worker-managers are more apt to take a traditionally more conservative view of interest rates and loans, particularly the quality of such loans. There is undoubtedly some compromise between these two views within the banking organization. But the degree and importance of such compromises are difficult to estimate. The easing of restrictions on interunit financing and recent provisions for the discount of commercial bills originating in the socialist sector seem to indicate that the representatives of socialist firms have influence on affairs hitherto considered banking's special preserves. It is of course true that such provisions and the easing of restrictions have at the same time increased banking's influence in the economy.

9.

MONEY, PRICES, AND VELOCITY

MONEY SUPPLY

When Yugoslavia abandoned the Soviet type of planning apparatus, money began to play an important role in economic activity. The former concept of the money supply defined in such a way as to include only coin and paper money was inadequate in a country that considered decentralization seriously. By the beginning of 1952 a new definition more consistent with the new economic system was agreed upon.[1] Since 1952 the money supply has been defined to include all monetary means that can be used directly as a means of payment, such as coin, paper money, transfer accounts of enterprises, liquid assets in investment funds, and other monetary assets such as savings deposits that can be readily converted. Such a definition, however, does not establish a clear-cut division between liquid and nonliquid assets. The vast middle ground between these two types of assets is a growing source of concern for the country's money managers.

Money supply estimates are derived by combining statistical and accounting data from banks. The justification for such an approach is that only banks can create monetary resources in the country. The liability side of the balance sheets of banks provides the monetary sources, and the asset side the means for their creation. Since other items such as compensation accounts, cash,

[1] D. Dimitrijević, "Faktori monetarnih kretanja" and "Naša novčana mase" ("Monetary Flow Factors" and "Our Stock of Money") *Glasnik narodne banke* ("Bulletin of National Bank"), no. 1 (1959), pp. 3–14 and 15–18, respectively.

and balances due to and due from banks also appear in their balance sheets, items on both sides of the balance sheet must first be balanced out before individual items can be classified into liquid and nonliquid assets. For 1959 these operations yielded the results presented in Table 14. The money consisted of sight liabilities plus notes and coin in circulation and was equal to 873 billion dinars. Nonliquid assets consisted of restricted and inactive deposits plus foreign exchange accounts of enterprises and counterpart funds and were equal to 649 billion dinars. The money supply and nonliquid assets constitute the "total monetary resources" in the economy.

The distribution of the money supply as presented in Table 15 suggests the growing importance of money in the economy. By 1957–59 the largest increases were registered in the cash balances of households and investors. In effect, consumers and investors are obtaining more of the means with which to influence the formation and distribution of income and wealth.

A closer examination of the country's monetary situation suggests that it is far from ideal if judged by income developments. The evidence summarized in Table 16 indicates that in the period 1952–59 the money supply increased by over two and one-half times while income only doubled. The situation is even worse when account is taken of the total monetary resources, which have increased almost fourfold. Special factors such as significant institutional changes may well have been the generators of such an increase in monetary resources.

According to Miloš Vučković, the main and almost sole reason for the expansion in the money supply has been the increase in the volume of short-term credits extended by the banking system.[2] Vučković estimates the increases in short-term bank credit to have been from 714 billion dinars in 1952 to 1,329 billion dinars in 1958 to 2,061 billion dinars in 1961. In effect, between 1952 and 1958 short-term bank credit almost doubled, and between 1952 and 1961 it almost tripled.

[2] "The Recent Development of the Money and Banking System of Yugoslavia," *Journal of Political Economy*, Aug. 1963, pp. 363–67.

TABLE 14. Consolidated balance sheet of all banks, December 31, 1959–December 31, 1962 (*in billions of dinars*)

	1959	1960	1961	1962
Assets				
Gold and foreign exchange	16	13	20	32
Total credits	1,554	1,824	2,067	2,479
Credits to enterprises for working assets	1,099	1,252	1,440	1,586
Consumer credits (through the banks)	80	96	135	177
Credits to government	156	176	270	467
Credits to investment funds	159	220	144	163
Other credits	60	81	78	86
Foreign assets	21	17	30	26
Other assets	21	43	54	89
TOTAL ASSETS	1,611	1,897	2,171	2,626
Liabilities				
Restricted and inactive deposits	529	596	746	803
Funds of banks	33	36	39	54
Reserve funds of enterprises	85	104	96	116
Government deposits	71	66	170	103
Blocked deposits of investors	154	188	216	233
Blocked deposits of investment funds	93	84	75	69
Foreign deposits in dinars	26	39	37	35
Other	67	79	113	193
Foreign exchange accounts of enterprises	52	46	52	36
Counterpart funds	113	92	100	138
Foreign liabilities	44	58	57	61
Sight liabilities	697	912	970	1,307
Giro accounts of enterprises	140	128	150	309
Liabilities to households	67	90	124	155
Government deposits	61	126	85	102
Liquid deposits of investors	183	197	168	221
Liquid deposits of investment	34	33	21	58
Liabilities to social organizations	15	—	—	—
Other sight liabilities	146	228	312	351
Resources in transit (floating)	51	110	110	108
Notes and coins in circulation	176	193	246	284
TOTAL LIABILITIES	1,611	1,897	2,171	2,626

Source: For 1959, National Bank of Yugoslavia, *Annual Report 1959*, p. 62; for 1960–62, Research Department, National Bank of Yugoslavia.

TABLE 15. Distribution of money supply by purpose of expenditures, 1957–62 (*end of year estimates in billions of dinars*)

Type of expenditures	Amounts						Structure in percentage of total money supply					
	1957	*1958*	*1959*	*1960*	*1961*	*1962*	*1957*	*1958*	*1959*	*1960*	*1961*	*1962*
Giro accounts of enterprises	128	119	140	128	150	309	18.5	16.5	16.0	11.6	12.3	19.5
Monetary resources of households	159	189	243	283	370	439	22.8	26.2	27.8	25.6	30.4	27.6
Government deposits	41	49	61	126	85	102	5.8	6.8	7.0	11.4	7.0	6.4
Investment funds	185	166	217	230	189	279	26.7	23.0	24.9	20.8	15.6	17.6
Monetary resources of social organizations & institutions	20	11	15	—	—	—	2.9	1.6	1.7	—	—	—
Items in transit (floating)	69	67	51	110	110	108	10.0	9.3	5.9	10.0	9.0	6.8
Unclassified monetary resources	92	120	146	228	312	351	13.3	16.6	16.7	20.6	25.7	22.1
Total	693	721	873	1,105	1,216	1,588	100.0	100.0	100.0	100.0	100.0	100.0

Source: National Bank of Yugoslavia, *Annual Report 1959*, p. 36, and, for 1960–62, Research Department, National Bank of Yugoslavia.

TABLE 16. Money, income, and monetary velocity, 1952–62

	1952	1953	1954	1955	1956	1957	1958	1959	1960	1961	1962
I. Money supply *	320	307	412	410	553	693	721	873	1105	1216	1588
Nonliquid assets	96	181	270	397	490	539	633	694	734	898	977
Total monetary volume	416	498	682	807	1040	1232	1354	1567	1839	2114	2565
II. National income †	1051	1258	1243	1455	1444	1780	1811	2130	2249	2341	—
III. Monetary velocity											
National income ÷ Money supply	3.25	4.09	3.01	3.54	2.43	2.56	2.51	2.55	2.04	1.93	—

* In billions of dinars, end of year figures, from National Bank of Yugoslavia, *Annual Reports* for years 1955–59.
† In billions of dinars and in 1956 prices, from *Statistički godišnjak 1961*, p. 98.

The principal beneficiaries of this credit expansion have been economic organizations engaged in industry, mining, and trade (internal and external) .[3] One reason for such an increase in short-term credit is that the various socialist firms resort to short-term bank credit as a means of supplementing their own long-term investment resources. The various restrictions imposed by the authorities during the 1950's on the use of investment funds by firms have prompted the firms to search for a substitute; this they have apparently found in the form of short-term bank credit. Moreover, there has been a tendency for worker-managers in socialist firms to use some of whatever investment funds are at their disposal to increase their personal incomes while at the same time resorting to short-term bank credit to make up the difference.

The idea of financing long-term projects with short-term funds is not new. Germany's industrialization was so financed during the 19th and the first half of the 20th centuries. Extensive renewals of short-term loans by German bankers meant in effect that they were financing long-term investment.[4] This type of financing, however, has not occurred in other capitalist countries such as Great Britain.

PRICES

The rapid expansion in the money supply coupled with the elimination of some of the more severe distortions in relative prices since 1952 produced as one of its consequences an increase in the general level of prices. Consider the cost of living index computed by the Federal Statistical Institute. The cost of living index presented in Table 17 is computed on the basis of average retail prices of goods and services gathered in 52 towns. The weights are derived from a family budget survey conducted in 1960 for four-member workers' and office employees' families.

The evidence summarized in Table 17 indicates that the cost of

[3] *Ibid.*
[4] Gerald M. Meier and Robert E. Baldwin, *Economic Development* (New York: John Wiley and Sons, 1962) , p. 96.

TABLE 17. Cost of living indexes, 1953–62 (Base: 1960 = 100)

	1953	1954	1955	1956	1957	1958	1959	1960	1961	1962
Cost of living index	70	69	77	83	85	90	91	100	108	118
Food	70	70	82	88	90	92	93	100	110	126
Tobacco and beverages	70	67	74	82	88	97	103	100	111	127
Clothing and footwear	99	89	95	96	97	101	100	100	103	108
Hygiene	75	77	82	84	85	94	95	100	115	126
Rent, water, and other	28	31	34	36	36	44	46	100	101	104
Fuel and lighting	52	54	58	61	66	69	75	100	107	111
Furnishings	90	87	100	103	100	99	98	100	106	108
Culture and recreation	69	75	77	82	80	95	97	100	118	127
Transportation, telegraph, and telephone	74	73	82	83	86	92	98	100	108	114
Other consumer goods	74	72	81	87	89	93	94	100	108	119
Other services	42	46	50	53	58	68	72	100	108	114

Source: *Statistički godišnjak 1962 and 1963*, pp. 243 (1962), 274 (1963).

living index increased by over 54 per cent in the period 1953–61 or by an average of 6 per cent per year. Every item contained in the index increased in price during this period. This increase applied even to such items as housing, tobacco, and utilities whose prices are governmentally controlled. Food prices, which are perhaps the best indication of free-market prices in the country, increased over 57 per cent during the period under review.

The wholesale price index for industrial products presented in Table 18 increased only 10 per cent from 1954 to 1961. The

TABLE 18. Wholesale price index for industrial products, 1954–62
(Base: 1960 = 100)

Year	Index number
1954	95
1955	97
1956	98
1957	98
1958	99
1959	98
1960	100
1961	105
1962	108

Source: *Statistički godišnjak 1962*, p. 240. The 1962 figures are from *Statistički godsšnjak 1963*, p. 273.

comparatively moderate rise in the prices of industrial products can be explained in part by the fact that industrial output almost doubled during this period. In addition, some of the items included in the index are under price controls. Finally, the method of computing the wholesale price index is such as to render any conclusions from it of doubtful value—at least for the purpose of gauging inflationary tendencies in the economy.

According to the explanation given by the Federal Statistical Institute, industrial prices are those prices at which producers sold their products on domestic wholesale markets. These prices do not take discounts into account, and they include the turnover tax as well as refunds for specific products provided by law. In effect, there appears to be a considerable amount of price rigging on the level of transactions from which wholesale price data are gathered.

The weights for the wholesale price index are derived from 1957 turnover data from enterprises selected according to their share of the total industrial output of the country. The specific criteria of importance, however, are not specified. It is stated that, insofar as the prices of manufactured products are concerned, 840 products from 620 selected enterprises are included, thereby accounting for at least 50 per cent of the turnover in every given branch of industry.[5] The prices of more than 100 agricultural products are included, and they are gathered from all agricultural cooperatives and economic organizations authorized to purchase products from private producers.[6]

VELOCITY

Monetary velocity and its determinants have received considerable attention in the economic literature of most countries. Until very recently, however, velocity, along with other aspects of monetary theory, has received very little attention from postwar Yugoslav economists. In view of the country's past economic arrangements, this is not particularly surprising. Emphasis on so-called real factors has shoved aside monetary analysis. It now appears that necessity has had its sobering effect, and monetary analysis is once again beginning to come into its own.[7] Some idea of the extent to which it is becoming fashionable is suggested by the number of works published in Yugoslavia in the field of monetary economics. The evidence is summarized in Table 19. The number of publications reached a peak in 1954 and then declined. But while the

---

[5] *Statistički godišnjak 1962*, p. 760.

[6] *Ibid.*

[7] Ivo Perišin, "Prilog analizi novčanih kretanja" ("The Contribution to Analyses of Monetary Flows"), *Ekonomski pregled* ("Economic Survey"), no. 1, 1961, pp. 1–39.

TABLE 19. Number of Yugoslav publications dealing with monetary economics, 1950–61

	1950	1951	1952	1953	1954	1955	1956	1957	1958	1959	1960	1961 *
Books and pamphlets	9	11	16	8	14	14	9	12	14	9	13	7
Articles and reviews	46	111	257	269	374	277	282	155	172	108	109	44

Source: "Bibliography on Monetary Economics," 1962, prepared for this writer by members of the faculty of economics, University of Belgrade, under the direction of Professor Dr. Miloš Vučković.
* First quarter only.

number declined the quality has improved, especially since 1956.

The money supply, national income, and income velocity estimates for the period 1952–59 are presented in Table 16. To judge from these estimates, income velocity rose sharply in 1953, declined, and then assumed a remarkable steadiness in the period 1956–59. Such behavior is about what one would expect during periods of uncertainty and rapid change in the organization of a country's economy. The reorganization was for the most part completed by 1956–59, and the uncertainty generated by such reorganization was reduced if not altogether eliminated.

The velocity estimates presented in Table 16 correspond very closely to those made by Ivo Perišin,[8] who gives the following velocities for 1952–58:

1952—2.7	1956—2.6
1953—3.2	1957—2.6
1954—2.8	1958—2.5
1955—3.4	

Perišin's estimates differ only because the national income estimates he used are in current prices rather than in 1956 prices. His estimates of the money supply are identical with those presented in Table 16.

[8] *Ibid.*, p. 20.

The determinants of income velocity continue to be the objects of a considerable amount of study—at least in the United States.[9] The equation of exchange approach to monetary theory owes much of its decline to the tendency on the part of some people to treat monetary velocity as though it were mechanically determined and empirically constant. The apparent failure of velocity to remain constant during the hectic period of the 1930's cast doubt on its mechanical determinants such as various payment arrangements and other institutional factors.

As a result, monetary theorists now approach the demand for money as an application of the general theory of choice. Thus the determinants of velocity can be expressed in terms of orthodox demand analysis (the price of the commodity, prices of related commodities, incomes, tastes, and expectations). And as Harry G. Johnson correctly points out, "Neither the quantity theory nor the Keynesian theory is what it was in the 1930's; in particular the modern quantity theorist is committed to neither full employment nor the constancy of velocity, and his theory is a theory of the relation between the stock of money and the level of money income, that is, a theory of velocity and not a theory of prices and employment." [10]

What does the behavior of velocity depend upon? In the sophisticated version of the quantity theory of money the behavior of velocity depends upon a number of factors.[11] Briefly, it depends upon equity yields (r_e), bond yields (r_b), the rate of change in prices $1/P\,(dP/dt)$, the fraction of wealth that people hold in the form of property (W), their real income (Y/P), and other factors considered by people as imparting utility to money. In symbols:

[9] See, for example, the various essays in Milton Friedman, ed., *Studies in the Quantity Theory of Money* (Chicago: University of Chicago Press, 1956), and George Macesich, "Determinants of Monetary Velocity in Canada, 1926–58," *Canadian Journal of Economics and Political Science*, May 1962, pp. 245–54. A summary of various monetary studies is contained in Harry G. Johnson, "Monetary Theory and Policy," *American Economic Review*, June 1962, pp. 335–85.

[10] *Op. cit.*, p. 344.

[11] Milton Friedman, "The Quantity Theory of Money—A Restatement," in Friedman, ed., *Studies in the Quantity Theory of Money*, pp. 3–21.

$$Y= V(r_e, r_b, \frac{1}{P}\frac{dP}{dt}, W, \frac{Y}{P}, u) \cdot M$$

where

Y = Money income
M = Stock of money
V = Velocity.

In short, the behavior of velocity depends upon the costs of holding money, the level of income, and wealth.

Recently Milton Friedman has argued that the behavior of velocity is influenced more by a long-term level of income that people can expect than by income that is currently received.[12] His view is, for example, that the contradiction indicated in the secular decline of velocity in the United States is more apparent than real. Thus, if velocity is computed with permanent income in the numerator rather than measured income, it remains unchanged in cyclical periods. Since measured income is presumably above permanent income at cyclical peaks and below permanent income at cyclical troughs, the positive conformity of measured velocity to cyclical changes of income may accordingly reflect differences between measured and permanent income.

Richard T. Selden argues that, as in the theory of consumer choice, the demand for money is influenced by the existence of substitutes and complements. Hypothesized substitutes for money may fall into three broad categories: liquid assets, negotiated options to borrow, and access to credit markets.[13] He adopts the definition used by Roland N. McKean that money complements are maturing debts since they require the holding of cash balances.[14] The numerical counterpart in monetary analysis to the price of substitutes for money can be considered as the differential between rates on long- and short-term loans. According to Selden,

[12] "The Demand for Money: Some Theoretical and Empirical Results," *Journal of Political Economy*, Aug. 1959, pp. 327–51.

[13] "Monetary Velocity in the United States," in Friedman, ed., *Studies in the Quantity Theory of Money*, p. 208.

[14] *Ibid.*

a rise in the differential implies an increase in the cost of money complements. The net effect will be an increase in the demand for money. If the differential falls, the converse holds true.[15]

Other investigators have tested the hypothesis that the behavior of velocity is influenced mainly by the cost of holding money as reflected in interest rates unadjusted for the yield in money.[16] Although they tend to agree that such a relationship exists, they dispute its significance as well as the type of interest rate (short or long term) to be used to measure the cost of holding money. A number of investigators also disagree as to the type of velocity that is appropriately related to the cost of holding money. Some theorists favor the narrower income velocity, whereas others favor the broader transactions velocity. Since these two velocities are not always proportional, the disagreement is not trivial.

To judge from studies made on the American economy, attempts to explain the behavior of velocity by such variables as the cost of holding money and the price of money substitutes have not been very successful. If we take these results seriously, velocity is not highly sensitive to changes, for example, in "the" rate of interest—at least for the range of interest rates examined in the American studies. My own work on Canadian velocity from 1926 to 1958 indicates that the cost of holding money, the cost of money substitutes, the real per capita disposable income, and the rate of change in prices are not significant determinants of the observed behavior of income velocity.[17]

Let us now consider the theoretical explanation for observed velocity behavior advanced by Friedman. The explanation derived from his permanent income hypothesis concentrates on the meaning attached to income and prices. In this view money holdings are adapted to permanent income and prices rather than the measured income and prices provided by statisticians. The relation between

---

[15] This argument and conclusion are disputed by David Meiselman ("Term Structure of Interest Rates" [unpublished doctoral dissertation, University of Chicago, 1961], pp. 74 ff.) .

[16] For a summary, see Selden, *op. cit.,* p. 196.

[17] Macesich, "Determinants of Monetary Velocity in Canada, 1926–58," pp. 245–54.

measured and permanent magnitudes is readily available in the work of Friedman; it need not be reported here.

The distinction between permanent and measured magnitudes can rationalize a part of the observed secular and cyclical behavior of income velocity in the United States in terms of a movement along a stable demand curve for money. Thus in Friedman's view income velocity does not behave in an erratic and unpredictable manner. It reflects shifts along a relatively stable demand schedule for money produced by changes in the variables entering into that schedule. An important implication of the American results is that most of the variation in measured velocity appears to be consistent with stable functional relations. If correct, one consequence of this finding is that measured income may be highly sensitive to changes in the stock of money.

The results of Canadian experience appear to be consistent with the permanent income hypothesis. Indeed, these results imply a strict quantity theory of the simplest kind for all permanent magnitudes in Canada,[18] thus suggesting that in Canada as in the United States measured income may be sensitive to changes in the stock of money.

In Yugoslavia monetary analysis has yet to reach this degree of sophistication, though the recent changes in the economy will undoubtedly lead to such sophistication. Velocity is still treated as though it were mechanically determined. The list of factors influencing velocity which is usually presented in Yugoslav literature bears some resemblance to that discussed by Irving Fisher.[19] Thus Dimitrija Dimitrijević, for example, lists four factors as influencing velocity in Yugoslavia in the years from 1952 to 1961: credit-monetary factors, effects of economic decentralization, regulations on expenditures, and external economic relations.[20]

In the first group of factors Dimitrijević considers as most

[18] George Macesich, "The Permanent Income Hypothesis and Canadian Monetary Velocity, 1935–58" (MS, 1962), and Friedman, "The Demand for Money," pp. 327–51.

[19] *The Purchasing Power of Money* (New York: Macmillan, 1913), pp. 79 ff.

[20] "Factori monetarnih kretanja" ("Monetary Flow Factors"), *Glasnik narodne banke* ("Bulletin of National Bank"), no. 1 (1959), pp. 3–14.

important the prohibition against interenterprise financing and the requirement that all payments within the socialist sector be made through the banking system. Both of these factors are viewed as having the effect of reducing velocity. They are roughly analogous to Fisher's "systems of payments in the community" category.

Economic decentralization in Yugoslavia has had the effect, among other things, of increasing the number of investment funds and redistributing the means of payment in favor of presumably high hoarders, thereby reducing velocity. In effect, a structural change has occurred in the economy so that high hoarders are now relatively more important; hence the demand for money has increased and velocity consequently decreased.

Various regulations on expenditures have had the effect of reducing velocity by forcing the holding of money, particularly by economic enterprises. Thus not only is a firm forbidden to lend to another, but under some circumstances it cannot draw on available deposits for its own use. For example, a firm may have more than a sufficient amount on deposit for the purchase of product A but not enough for the purchase of product B. It cannot on its own initiative transfer deposits earmarked for the purchase of A to the purchase of B. The various regulations take on the character of quality credit controls familiar in the postwar period in the United States. They are also similar to various blocked accounts that characterized European trade during the 1930's.

Yugoslavia's external economic position as characterized by its unfavorable balance of trade constitutes a special set of factors slowing down velocity. The excess of imports over exports has had the effect of absorbing the domestic means of payment into special funds held by high hoarders. Thus the familiar counterpart fund whereby domestic means of payment are used to purchase such commodities as American agricultural surpluses is a case in point. Dimitrijević estimates that at the end of 1952 there were 27 billion dinars in the counterpart fund, but by the end of September 1958 the fund contained 146 billion dinars.[21] For all practical purposes

[21] *Ibid.*, p. 12.

these counterpart funds constitute blocked accounts, the expenditure of which is very closely regulated. They are used primarily to pay the expenses of foreign staffs in Yugoslavia.

MONETARY CONTROLS

Although the influence of money in the economy has increased, especially in the last three years, and it is expected to increase even more, its influence is still not as great as it is in the free-market type of economy. In this context Yugoslavia falls somewhere between the East with its fully planned economies and the West with its relatively free economies. Thus the country maintains economic planning together with a degree of freedom on the part of individual economic units. Consequently its system can best be described as a mixture of two apparently opposite elements.

The purpose of the economic plan as noted elsewhere in this study is to provide and implement the general line of economic policy with particular emphasis on the rate and pattern of economic development. The relatively high degree of freedom of individual economic units has the objective of ensuring optimal economic behavior on the part of consumers and producers. The monetary and nonmonetary institutions and measures attempt to achieve a smooth interaction between these two opposites. Such are the characteristics that distinguish the Yugoslav economy from other economies which place emphasis on one element or another.

The combination of economic planning and a free market is indicated by the purposive roles played by money and credit in the economy. Monetary assets, whether liquid or nonliquid, and their sources of credit must be used for predetermined purposes such as investment and current operations. Even within such broad categories, the use of these resources is further restricted for specific activities such as, for example, the improvement of housing and the replacement or improvement of roads. These restrictions, which were imposed to meet the requirements of economic planning, resulted in situations in which an economic unit had a surplus in one account and a shortage in another without any means of transferring surplus resources.

The purposive character of money and credit should be regarded as a transitional stage in a process of giving money an increasingly influential role—a process which started when the fully centralized type of economic planning was abandoned. In the period 1956–61 the purposive division of monetary resources became less marked, and in 1961 many of the former restrictions were eliminated, especially as they pertained to the operation of economic enterprises, which are now free to spend their funds as they see fit.

Another restriction, though it is not purposive in character, is a consequence of economic planning in the distribution of the national product. With the exception of consumer credits granted in the course of retail trade, economic units are prohibited from interunit financing. Economic units may or may not use their resources, but they are not allowed to lend them to others. Radical changes, however, are already on the way. Interenterprise financing of some investment projects, the establishment of special associations by groups of enterprises for the purpose of financing other units, and the extension of credit from ten or twenty days to two months for the purchase and sale of goods point to the decreasing importance of restrictions on interunit financing.

An important distinguishing feature of the Yugoslav system, and indeed in all systems with elements of economic planning, is the requirement that every economic unit within the socialist sector must hold all of its monetary resources in appropriate accounts with a prescribed bank and perform all banking operations through that bank. Each economic enterprise is required to effect all payments through accounts with that bank and to apply to it for all funds except investment funds, which are granted by investment loan funds. Such funds are to be used through accounts held with the bank administering the investment loan fund. The purpose of these restrictions is to make it possible to obtain a full record of the monetary transactions of economic units in the socialist sector and so provide a means for checking their transactions against legal enactments. At the same time that this restriction provides a check on the legality of monetary transactions, it also provides a very powerful means for controlling the money supply and the volume of credit by the central bank.

This control measure is supplemented by the central bank's power to grant credit to other banks and to change the reserve ratio of these banks. For example, in 1961 the reserve ratio of communal banks was 30 per cent. Attempts were recently made by the National Bank to base credit policy on the interest rate as the main regulatory instrument, but these were given up when this policy had adverse effects on such favored industries as the metallurgical, electrical engineering, and building industries. The Yugoslavs are willing to postpone central bank control by way of influence on interest rates until the newly established postwar industries are in a position to withstand the rigors of such a policy. Until then the central bank apparently prefers the more direct approach in dealing with problems of regulating money and credit.

Changes in banking and credit laws on March 1, 1961, were apparently motivated by a desire to obtain a more effective control over monetary matters; these were rapidly getting out of hand as evidenced by price rises. Indeed, the promulgation of these changes in banking and credit laws was accompanied by a declaration in the Federal Assembly by the State Secretary of the Treasury that the changes were made primarily "to prevent the issue of superfluous money." [22] Several important principles regarding monetary matters were established by these changes, namely, that general credit policy should be defined by the Federal Social Plan in accordance with the general line of planned development; that a general credit plan must be prepared by the National Bank for the whole banking system; that the discount rate and legal reserve requirements should be operated in a more flexible manner than before; that bills of exchange, promissory notes, obligations, and cashier's notes should be introduced; and that the policy of activating or neutralizing components of the money supply should be better coordinated with fluctuations in the demand and supply of commodities.[23]

[22] Vučković, op. cit.
[23] Ibid.

10.

INVESTMENT

DEMAND FOR AND SUPPLY OF INVESTMENT FUNDS

Investment is usually considered to be one of the key variables in all dynamic economies. The methods for financing and allocating investment to competing ends, however, are not homogeneous. They are essentially a function of the economic system in force. The spectrum of these methods ranges from those employed in free-market economies that emphasize the market mechanism to those of fully centralized economies that emphasize direct administrative allocation of investment resources. In between these two extremes there are various combinations. One such combination is that currently employed in Yugoslavia which attempts to combine central decision making with emphasis on the market mechanism through the media of individual economic units for allocating investment resources.

There are three main sources for financing investment projects in Yugoslavia.[1] One is the federal investment fund. The second is the investment funds of republic and local authorities. The third is the investment funds of the economic enterprises. These three sources are supplied by means of various taxes, legally established shares in the income of economic activity by federal, republic, and local levels of government, private savings, public loans, and foreign loans and grants.

[1] B. Kubović and V. Tričković, *National and Regional Economic Planning in Yugoslavia* (Belgrade: Federal Planning Bureau, 1961), p. 18.

Personal income taxes, personal savings, and public loans have not been important sources of supply for investment funds. The low per capita income, which amounted to approximately $300 in 1958, is at least partly responsible for this lack of importance.[2] In addition, the government is reluctant to rely too heavily on private sources for funds. Two national loans were instituted in the difficult years of 1948 and 1950; these brought in about 9 billion dinars.[3] These loans were for the most part redeemed by 1958. In 1954 economic enterprises were required to raise a loan out of their own funds for the purpose of financing the General Investment Fund on the federal level. By 1958 these funds had largely been returned to the enterprises.

Foreign loans and grants have been important in supplying the economy with investment resources. In the period 1952–56, for example, such loans and grants accounted for almost 33 per cent of the total value of investments in that period.[4] These funds were obtained for the most part from Western countries and principally from the United States.

Unlike the situation in the years when the economy was fully centralized, the federal budget is no longer used as a principal source for investment financing. Investment monies accumulated through various taxes on economic activity and amortization funds are earmarked and placed at the disposal of various investment funds. This avoids the difficulties that previously arose out of budget financing when discontinuity in investment resulted from continuous revisions of regional forecasts in order to meet more immediate and pressing needs. Assurance of permanent sources of receipts for the various investment funds now provides a continuity to investment projects hitherto lacking.

In 1957 there were some forty investment funds at the firm, communal, republic, and federal levels. The bulk of the money in these funds is earmarked for economic investment. Table 20

[2] Augustin Papić, "Investment Financing in Yugoslavia," *Annals of Collective Economy,* April–Nov. 1959, p. 211.

[3] *Ibid.*

[4] *Ibid.,* p. 210.

TABLE 20. Principal investment funds in 1957 (*in billions of dinars*)

Fund	Assets	Amount used
Social investment funds	248.1	197.1
Housing construction funds	66.2	48.8
Special social funds	34.6	34.6
Budget	19.1	19.1
Investment funds of state and institutional organizations	28.0	23.7
Miscellaneous funds	9.8	2.2
Investment funds of enterprises	70.7	73.2
Net investments (new)	476.5	398.7
Amortization funds	132.1	88.7
Gross investments	609.1	487.4

Source: Augustin Papič, "Investment Financing in Yugoslavia," *Annals of Collective Economy*, April–Nov. 1959, p. 214.

summarizes for 1957 the principal investment funds and their resources.

Social investment funds are the principal group, and they are established at the local, republic, and federal levels. The distribution of these resources among the three levels of government is summarized in Table 21. These funds receive their resources in

TABLE 21. Distribution of investment funds in 1957 by levels of government, federal, republic, and local (*in billions of dinars*)

Level of government	Assets		Utilization	
	AMOUNT	PER CENT PARTICIPATION	AMOUNT	PER CENT PARTICIPATION
General Investment Fund (federal)	162.9	65.7	140.3	71.2
Investment funds of republic	26.4	10.6	15.6	7.9
Local investment funds	58.8	23.7	41.2	20.9

Source: Same as Table 20.

part from economic enterprises before and after the net income of the enterprise is determined. Another part is received from the allocation of resources by one investment fund to another and from foreign capital invested in the country.

The construction of dwellings as well as other works of a local character is financed from a construction fund. Funds are obtained by requiring economic enterprises and other organizations to pay a fixed percentage of the organization's wage bill.

The development of various types of economic activity such as agriculture, construction, and industry is encouraged by the use of resources from the special social funds. Money from these funds is used chiefly to train personnel, conduct research, and in general promote activity considered to be stimulating to the various sectors of the economy.

Budgets of the local, republic, and federal levels of government are used in the traditional manner, including the promotion of education, public health, and welfare as well as the construction of public buildings. The various state agencies and institutions are provided with investment funds to renew their fixed assets.

Economic enterprises have two principal sources for investment financing. One is the "liquid assets of the fixed capital funds" (depreciation) and consumption funds. These constitute the net income of each enterprise. Such resources can be used for new investments. The other is the amortization fund, whose resources are earmarked for the maintenance of fixed capital assets, though they can sometimes be used for enlarging an enterprise.

With the exception of the special investment funds, which are administered directly by the banks, all funds are legal entities and are administered by management committees.

Since the decentralization reforms of 1952, and especially since 1953 when the resources at the disposal of economic enterprises and local levels of government were enlarged, a significant reduction has occurred in the role that republic and federal agencies play in the investment of funds. The increasing role of the communes in the investment field was discussed in Chapter 2.

ALLOCATION OF INVESTMENT FUNDS

The planning of investment is an integral part of the country's economic system. Investments are planned between sectors and within sectors of the economy. Such planning constitutes one of the principal methods whereby the planner's influence is exerted on the economy.[5]

In order to obtain investment resources for new projects or for major reconstruction, economic enterprises on the local levels of government must apply to the Federal Investment Bank for a substantial part of such resources. These resources are earmarked for the various sectors of the economy on the basis of sector projections contained in the intermediate economic plan.[6] The Investment Bank through its branches announces that it is accepting bids from economic enterprises and other organizations for the earmarked resources. It grants these resources to applicants and their projects on the basis of such economic criteria as the profitability of the project, the amount of money needed per unit of capacity, the length of the borrowing period, and the balance-of-payment effects of the project. In addition, the applicant is required to provide resources to cover part of the cost of the project. This is an opportunity for the allocation of those investment resources at the disposal of enterprises and local authorities. The important role played by the General Investment Fund in the implementation of the planned volume and composition of investment is indicated by the fact that projects of national significance as well as those expected to speed up the economic development of the country's underdeveloped areas are financed exclusively out of this fund.[7]

Annual economic plans are another important factor influenc-

[5] See also Egon Neuberger, "The Yugoslav Investment Auctions," *Quarterly Journal of Economics,* Feb. 1959, pp. 80–115, and his "Central Banking in Semi-planned Economies—Yugoslav Case" (unpublished doctoral dissertation, Harvard University, 1957).

[6] Kubović and Tričković, *op. cit.,* p. 18.

[7] *Ibid.*

ing the allocation of investment resources. These plans, which may change from year to year in accordance with requirements of longer-term plans, may contain specific provisions as to the rates at which the various decentralized funds, such as, for example, construction funds and the enterprise's amortization funds, can be utilized.

An opportunity for political criteria to influence the allocation of investment resources is provided by federal law. The law grants to the various levels of government the right of decision on any project. They have, however, seldom exercised the right.[8]

Although much remains to be done, these changes in the method of allocating investment funds represent significant steps toward a more rational and efficient utilization of the country's resources. The situation now contrasts strikingly with that which prevailed during 1945–52, when the country experimented with central planning.[9] At that time investment resources obtained through the federal budget were allocated without obligation to repay on the part of recipients. Some types of investment projects such as railroads, airports, seaports, roads, education, public health, and welfare are still in a favored position in that they are not obliged to return borrowed resources with interest. Most investment projects, however, are now required to meet the tests of economic criteria or else fall by the wayside.

The present system for allocating investment resources is one phase of the new economic system with its emphasis on the decentralization of economic activity. Increased responsibility has been placed on individuals, enterprises, and local levels of government for the rational and efficient utilization of investment resources. Incentives to this end are incorporated in the contracts between enterprises and banks. These contracts contain provisions to the effect that if expenditures should be increased during the execution of the project and additional work incurred the costs are to be borne by the enterprises. Conversely, if savings are made in the course of executing the project, such savings go to the credit of

8 Papić, *op. cit.*, p. 220.
9 *Ibid.*

the enterprises. They can, for example, use these savings for additional investment in such critical areas as housing.

Another provision of the contract requiring repayment within a specified time has eliminated the monotonous delays in the completion of projects which were so prevalent under the old system. In the event that income from the project is insufficient to repay funds borrowed or if the project is not completed in the specified time, the repayment is extracted from other resources of the enterprise or from the resources of the local underwriters such as communes and districts.

A further incentive toward economy is provided by the fact that the enterprise is required to deposit with the bank a guarantee of about 5 per cent of the total value of the loan. This is returned to it upon completion of the project and repayment of the loan. If the additional expenditures exceed this amount, the enterprise is required to supply additional resources. In situations in which the division of responsibility between enterprises and planning office or contractor for the execution of a project is not clearly defined, difficulties arise. Attempts to remove some of these difficulties by placing more responsibility on the contractor have met with a measure of success.

The setting of interest rates and repayment times, study of the profitability of a project, and cost sharing are important measures designed to instill responsibility and initiative at the firm and local levels. At the same time these measures provide the economic planners with a way to guide investment in the economy. In this connection nominal interest rates have not been particularly important. The nominal rates are for the most part unrealistic and range from 2 per cent for electrification projects and research and development to 4 per cent in industry and mining, with 3 per cent in agriculture, forestry, construction, transport, and commerce.[10]

Federal regulations fix maximum repayment periods. These periods vary from 10 to 30 years except in the cases of electric power projects, which may be extended to 50 years. As a rule,

---

[10] *Ibid.*, pp. 223–24.

however, the length of the repayment period is decided upon by negotiation between the enterprise and the bank with shorter periods receiving decidedly more favorable consideration by the banks.[11] The net effect is to bring investment periods within more realistic time horizons.

Participation of the enterprise is an important element in the allocation of investment resources since the resources of the special investment fund and particularly the General Investment Fund are inadequate to take care of the current investment effort. While such participation provides the investor with an incentive to think through his project carefully and in effect is a factor influencing the effective as distinct from the nominal interest rate, it also serves as a signal to enterprises indicating to them those fields of investment most favored by the country's planners. At the same time these participation funds serve to supplement the General Investment Fund. In 1958, for example, they amounted to 27 per cent of the monies paid out by the Fund.[12] Participation funds from enterprises are negligible in such favored projects as power and mining. In other sectors of the economy they become very important. In agriculture such participation varies between 10 and 40 per cent, in industry between 20 and 80 per cent, in construction between 10 and 30 per cent, in transportation between 20 and 50 per cent, in commerce and tourist trades between 30 and 50 per cent. These are minimum rates and more favorable credit terms are granted to those enterprises which offer higher participation rates. And enterprises in the underdeveloped areas of the country receive even more favorable consideration.

POSTWAR INVESTMENT PROGRAM: A SUMMARY
AND AN APPRAISAL

Aside from the reconstruction period, which according to some estimates lasted until 1947, the country's postwar investment program falls roughly into two distinct periods. The first period is that of 1947–52 and the second since 1953. Large-scale investments

[11] *Ibid.*, p. 224.
[12] *Ibid.*

in industry coupled with a centrally administered economy characterize the first period. An economic blockade by the Eastern European countries together with severe droughts in 1950 and 1952 brought an end to the first period. The second period, since 1953, is still characterized by large-scale investments in industry but with a significantly changed economic system and method for marshaling and allocating investment funds. Throughout both periods the structure of the economy has continued to change from that of an agricultural to an industrial economy; by 1958 industry and mining accounted for 42 per cent of the national income and agriculture for 28 per cent, with the agricultural population amounting to a little over 50 per cent as compared to the prewar figure of almost 78 per cent.[13]

A comparison of the volume and direction of investments in prewar and in postwar Yugoslavia is instructive in the preference given industry. If the available estimates can be trusted, in the period between 1923 and 1939 net investments in the country's national income amounted to roughly 4 per cent, while in the period between 1947 and 1958 these investments averaged approximately 23 per cent.[14] Table 22 summarizes the structure of these investments in the prewar and postwar periods. Categories labeled in the table as economic and noneconomic investments are distinguished by the fact that the former are arbitrarily defined to include all investments designed to increase the country's production capacity and the latter to include such nonproductive activities as public services, education, and housing.

As a result of the rapid growth of national income since 1953 the proportion of net investment to the total national income has tended to fall. Thus in the years from 1947 to 1949 investment stood at almost 27 per cent of national income, but by 1957–58 the figure had declined to slightly more than 20 per cent. The percentage of net investments is summarized in Table 23.

In the immediate postwar period so-called noneconomic investments received considerable emphasis in Yugoslavia's investment program owing to the need to reconstruct the devastating damages

[13] *Yugoslav Survey,* April 1960, p. 35.
[14] *Ibid.,* p. 38.

TABLE 22. Structure of investments according to purpose (*percentages of average shares*)

	Net investments		Gross investments	
	1923–39	1947–58	1959–62	1953–62
Total	100	100	100	100
Economic investments	64	78	74	76
Industry	15	45	37	38
Agriculture	19	7	11	11
Transport and communication	24	21	16	16
Other economic investments	6	5	10	11
Noneconomic investments	36	22	26	24
Housing construction	28	11	15	13
Other noneconomic investments	8	11	11	10

Source: *Yugoslav Survey*, April 1960, p. 38. The 1959–62 and 1953–62 figures are from the Research Department, National Bank of Yugoslavia.

resulting from the war. At the same time the rapid population shifts from agriculture to industry aggravated the situation and required substantial expenditures for housing, education, and public services. Thereafter the program emphasis was placed on the construction of projects considered to be keys to further economic development. These were favored largely at the expense

TABLE 23. National income and net investments, 1947–58 (*average yearly amounts in billions of dinars in 1956 prices*)

	1947–49	1950–52	1953–56	1957–58	Average over entire period
National income	1,118.5	1,116.2	1,364.6	1,754.8	1,306.0
Net investments in fixed assets	299.5	286.7	294.6	357.4	304.3
Proportion of net investments to the national income, in %	26.8	25.7	21.6	20.4	23.3

Source: *Yugoslav Survey*, April 1960, p. 38, and *Statistički godišnjak 1961*.

of such noneconomic investments as public services. Changes in the economic system whereby local authorities are empowered to undertake significant investments on their own initiative have resulted in a marked upsurge in noneconomic investments. This is particularly true in such critical fields as housing. Table 24 shows the division of total investment between economic and noneconomic categories.

A detailed examination of the distribution of investments, summarized in Table 25, confirms the casual observation that industry has been the most favored sector of the economy. Invest-

TABLE 24. Economic and noneconomic investments, 1947–58 (*average yearly amounts in billions of dinars at 1956 prices*)

	1947–49	1950–52	1953–56	1957–58	1947–58
Economic investments	260.6	285.5	310.3	369.6	310.5
Percentage of total investment	73.6	80.9	81.0	74.5	77.9
Noneconomic investments	93.6	67.6	73.0	126.8	85.8
Percentage of total investment	26.4	19.1	19.0	25.5	22.1
Total investment	354.2	353.1	383.3	496.4	396.3

Source: *Yugoslav Survey*, April 1960, p. 40.

ments in industry reached a peak in the period 1950–52. Thereafter it became possible to invest more in other sectors of the economy and as a consequence agriculture and transport received greater attention.

Investments in industry and mining rose steadily after 1947 and reached a peak of 215 billion dinars in 1952, or over 79 per cent of the total economic investment in the economy. By 1958 their share declined to less than 42 per cent. Such investments are justified by the Yugoslavs on the basis of the existence of large unexploited resources, particularly in hydroelectric power and in the various minerals, as well as the political tensions with Cominform countries that existed after 1948. The figures in Table 26 summarize the distribution of investments in industry. These figures show the

TABLE 25. Gross investments per industrial sector, 1947–58 (*average yearly investments in billions of dinars in 1956 prices*)

	1947–49		1950–52		1953–56		1957–58		1947–58	
	Amount	*%*	*Amount*	*%*	*Amount*	*%*	*Amount*	*%*	*Amount*	*%*
Industry	134.2	51.5	193.5	67.8	192.1	61.9	162.0	43.8	173.0	57.4
Agriculture	22.8	8.8	17.4	6.1	23.6	7.6	58.7	15.9	27.7	9.2
Forestry	8.8	3.4	3.3	1.2	5.7	1.8	6.6	1.8	6.0	2.0
Building	9.9	3.8	10.4	3.6	9.3	3.0	13.7	3.7	10.5	3.5
Transport	70.1	26.9	62.6	18.4	61.0	19.7	100.4	27.2	67.7	22.4
Commerce	13.4	5.1	7.1	2.5	15.7	5.1	23.2	6.3	14.2	4.7
Crafts	1.4	0.5	1.2	0.4	2.9	0.9	5.0	1.3	2.4	0.8
Total	260.6	100.0	285.5	100.0	310.3	100.0	369.6	100.0	310.5	100.0

Source: *Yugoslav Survey*, April 1960, p. 40.

emphasis placed on the generation of power, including that from water, coal, and oil. Ferrous metallurgical industries and the metal industries that are designated as basic industries also came in for favorable treatment. Nonferrous metallurgical industries received a strong boost between 1947 and 1954 with the construction of new plants for aluminum and copper production and in 1957 with the construction of new facilities for zinc production. Shipbuild-

TABLE 26. Distribution of investments in industry, 1947–58 (*average yearly share in percentages*)

	1947–49	1950–52	1953–56	1957–58	1947–58
Power generation	28.2	30.2	34.0	36.6	32.1
Basic industry	47.0	53.4	47.1	31.4	46.1
Processing industry	24.2	16.4	18.9	30.3	21.4
Unclassified	0.6	—	—	1.7	0.4
Total	100.0	100.0	100.0	100.0	100.0

Source: *Yugoslav Survey*, April 1960, p. 41.

ing and electrical equipment industries surged ahead under the favorable investment program. Particularly significant during the period since 1952 has been the development of a chemical industry with its emphasis on the production of artificial fibers. Other industries that received favorable treatment were the food- and timber-processing and textile industries. In addition, considerable funds were expended on the modernization of existing industrial facilities.

Until relatively recently the agricultural sector has been the country's stepchild. In the period between 1947 and 1958 agriculture received only 9.2 per cent of the gross investment in the economy. Prior to 1953 most of the investment was allocated to the construction of buildings and only a relatively small part was used for equipment and farm machinery. Since 1957, however, this policy has undergone significant changes, with the bulk of investments going into the acquisition of equipment and farm machinery. This change is rationalized by some as the consequence of the country's ability to produce its own farm machinery and thus conserve scarce foreign exchange. The figures in Table 27 summarize the structure of investments in agriculture.

Yugoslavia's transportation system was virtually wiped out dur-

TABLE 27. Technical structure of investments in agriculture, 1946–56 and 1957–58 (*in percentages*)

	1946–56 average	*1957–58* average
Building and other construction work	61.4	32.3
Equipment	21.0	45.9
Purchase of livestock	6.6	4.8
Seedlings	3.3	4.7
Other investments	7.7	12.3
Total	100.0	100.0

Source: *Yugoslav Survey*, April 1960, p. 42.

ing the war. After the war what had not been destroyed was outmoded and badly in need of repairs. Transportation therefore received high priority in the immediate postwar period. Railroad transport received most of the funds allocated for transportation. By 1957, however, a shift had occurred, and motor vehicles as well as other means of transportation such as airplanes and ships have since received favorable treatment.

Other sectors of the economy have come in for more favorable treatment of late. This is particularly true of forestry, building, commerce, and handicraft. But the most underdeveloped segment of the economy consists of the service trades, which are represented largely by private artisans conducting their operations under what can be called at best an "unfavorable tax structure." In fact, it is one whose objective is to eliminate the private artisans altogether.

The so-called noneconomic investments have once again begun to receive more favorable treatment in the allocation of investment funds. The largest part of the investment funds in this sector goes to housing construction and municipal projects. The results of investments in this sector are summarized in Table 28. Between 1947 and 1949 housing construction received favorable treatment. In 1950–52 it gave way to accelerated construction of projects considered to be key components of further development. Reorganization of the economic system after 1953 and the establish-

TABLE 28. Noneconomic investments, 1947–58 (*average yearly amounts in billions of dinars in 1956 prices*)

	1947–49	1950–52	1953–56	1957–58	1947–58
Housing-commercial * construction	52.4	38.1	47.2	85.1	52.6
Construction of cultural & social projects	20.4	16.6	15.5	18.0	17.4
Construction of office buildings	20.8	12.9	10.3	23.7	15.8

Source: *Yugoslav Survey*, April 1960, p. 43.
* Other than office buildings.

ment of special housing funds at local levels encouraged a speed-up in such construction. These funds, which are supplied by special taxes on personal income, have expanded with the growth of personal incomes. Investments in cultural and social projects have been fairly steady over the entire period. After 1956 the construction of office buildings received favorable treatment because of the rapid growth in the economy.

An objective evaluation of the country's investment efforts suggests that the economy is rapidly approaching the point where it will be incapable of adequately digesting the large-scale investments in industry. Although some Yugoslav economists disagree, there already appears to be insufficient utilization of existing industrial capacity. Such underutilization appears particularly serious in some of the most modern plants. Poor organization, unrealistic output norms, inferior quality and assortment of projects, high prices, and an inadequate number of qualified personnel are the principal reasons given for the underutilization of existing capacity.[15] One example will suffice to illustrate the point. Radio-Elektro in Kragujevac, Serbia, was on the verge of liquidation in 1960. Reorganization, redesign of its products, and changes in the composition of its work force, with emphasis placed on obtaining qualified personnel, increased output through October 1961 by 87 per cent over the entire year 1960, indicating almost a doubling of output for 1961 over 1960.[16] Indeed, the workers' management councilors of the enterprise decided to take part of their returns in the form of leisure by cutting their work week from six days to five and one-half.

The agriculture sector has suffered from the heavy investment priority given to industry and the resulting economic imbalance. Although agriculture showed signs of revival in 1953, it was not until 1957–60 that significant changes began to occur. At this time agriculture began to receive more favorable attention in the

[15] Two issues of *Eknonomski pregled* ("Economic Survey"), nos. 2 and 3 (1960), are devoted to an examination of problems arising out of weaknesses in the country's industrial output.

[16] *Politika* (Belgrade), Nov. 11, 1961.

allocation of investment funds, most of them going into mechanization. Other benefits have also flowed into this sector in recent years. Agricultural organizations, unlike enterprises in other sectors, are exempted from paying interest on their capital assets, and the rate is somewhat lower on working capital. The effect has been to strengthen agriculture. Much remains to be done, however, if this sector is to become something more than a drag on the economy.

The most pressing problem and perhaps the source of much of the existing imbalance in the economy is the quality of the human agent.[17] Even though the tempo of investment in the economy has been slowed down since 1952, it was reported in 1957 that manufacturing and mining have less than 50 per cent of the highly skilled workers and 80 per cent of the moderately skilled workers that they really need and that the training of workers is significantly behind current needs.[18] To this may be added that although the country has twice as many university students in terms of population as does Great Britain and five times as many as in 1939, the number of university students graduating each year is only 50 per cent of the country's current requirements. To judge by the amount of investment allocated to the improvement of the quality of the human agent, the importance of this factor in economic development is recognized in Yugoslavia.

All too often discussions of balance versus priorities in the investment program of various countries lead to the hopeless conclusion that nothing can be done until everything can be done. Critics of Yugoslav efforts should remember the Yugoslavian proverb which, roughly translated, says, "He who works makes mistakes." And on this score there are no more severe critics of some of the country's efforts than the Yugoslavs themselves—albeit the criticism is consistent with the country's institutional framework and its objective of "building socialism."

[17] See the interesting article dealing with the importance of the human agent in economic development by the Yugoslav economist Branko Horvat, "The Optimum Rate of Investment," *Economic Journal*, Dec. 1958, pp. 747–67.

[18] *Ibid.*, p. 760.

11.

INDUSTRY

Industrialization is almost universally considered an important means for achieving economic development. It is a way to raise the living standards and the per capita incomes of the people in the country. This is the usual justification for a country's embarking on a program of industrialization. Another reason advanced is that industrialization serves to diversify exports and increase the stability of foreign exchange earnings and national income. At the same time industrialization, which enables a country to produce and sell products competitively in the world market, increases the total of foreign exchange earnings and the national income. Still another justification for industrialization is that it gives employment to the unemployed or partially unemployed. This depends, of course, on conditions prevailing in other sectors of the economy. Moreover, the industrial projects in which these people are to be employed must be economically sound so as to make a net contribution to national income. Coupled with this justification is the fact that industrialization may also serve as a means for establishing domestic markets for such local raw materials as agricultural, timber, or mineral products which otherwise would be unused. If these human and natural resources are not used to their full economic potential, so the argument goes, economic losses occur to the economy. Whether or not this utilization provides a net gain to the economy depends on the costs and benefits flowing from any given industrial project. Often, however, such a justification over-looks the existence of complementarities among inputs.

Unfortunately major errors have been committed for the sake of industrialization and economic development. The obvious test of economic soundness for all projects is often forgotten by under-developed countries in their zeal to industrialize. Projects which fail to pass such tests occasion the loss of desperately needed resources. All too often these projects are sponsored by govern-ments and undertaken for purely political reasons. Far too many serve no other purpose than to boost national pride—an important goal, however. One way to avoid such blunders is, of course, for governments to refrain from direct investment in industry or, failing that, to insist on the principle that no project will be financed unless thorough investigation and analysis by qualified and impartial people show it to be economically, technically, and financially sound.

If too much weight is placed on self-sufficiency in its industriali-zation program, a country may be deprived of the benefits flowing from the international division of labor. This is particularly true for small countries. It is to their special interest to weigh carefully the principles of self-sufficiency and international specialization. Such countries can gain the most by emphasizing the export of products that they can produce at costs low enough to meet international competition while at the same time producing prod-ucts for domestic consumption at costs no higher than those of imported goods before duty. This consideration will preclude the establishment of industries merely to gain self-sufficiency. Although national income is maximized by participation in the international division of labor, such a guideline is no guarantee that a country will at the same time maximize the requirements of security and stability.

Another source of potential error may arise out of the argument that a certain industry should be established because of the exist-ence of suitable raw materials in a country. The economic signifi-cance of these raw materials, however, can only be ascertained by rigorous analysis of product costs attributable to the local raw materials and comparison with the costs elsewhere. If no other use exists for local materials, the justification for using them, and also labor, can be calculated in terms of national income profitability. In this calculation the project under consideration is charged for the raw material at its alternative economic value to the economy rather than at its commercial value.

Maurice Zenke has aptly summed up many of the common errors of industrialization:

The question that planners ask in Asia is not "How can the national income . . . be increased most at least cost?" Instead they begin from a whole series of different premises and build upon them. They argue that wealth comes from industrialization; so they create uneconomic industries and bolster them with protection. They accept that national safety requires a high degree of autarchy; so they build up defense industries which run expensively because their production is too low.[1]

Another common mistake in industrialization is the belief that heavy industry is the cornerstone of economic development in general and industrial development in particular. No matter what the cost, proponents of this view tend to argue, heavy industry must come first. The argument is derived from the belief that heavy industry supports other industries. This is true for the world as a whole. It is not true, however, for any given country and is especially incorrect for many underdeveloped countries. Their interests are better served by importing the products of such industries from the countries that produce for the world market. Underdeveloped countries with an adequate endowment of such natural resources as iron ore and coal can hope for a measure of success if a steel industry is under consideration. But this success will flow from the fact that the heavy industry in question was an economically sound project rather than that it fell in the category of heavy industry.

A country and its government may be well aware of the fact that, on strictly economic grounds, many of the industrial projects

[1] *Development for Free Asia* (London: Chatto and Windus, 1956) , p. 44.

undertaken are wobbly or even worse. Nevertheless, these projects are pushed forward on the ground that other factors such as defense, health, welfare, and even ideology outweigh economic considerations. If so, these projects should be understood for what they are. There is little point in rationalizing them on economic grounds only later to justify their failure on the same grounds.

THE PROBLEM OF CAPITAL- AND LABOR-INTENSIVE TECHNIQUES IN A DEVELOPING ECONOMY

An issue of particular concern to developing countries is whether they should use technology appropriate to their existing factor endowments (which normally means labor-intensive methods) or whether they should anticipate the relative growth of capital and immediately start to use capital-intensive methods even though such methods are inappropriate for their existing factor endowments.

The usual theoretical justification for using techniques appropriate to existing factor endowments is that an underdeveloped country will not use its limited resources best by imitating the techniques of developed countries. On the contrary, such countries should develop techniques appropriate to a thinner and wider spreading of their existing capital. The borrowing of technology from developed countries, in effect, wastes capital by spreading it too intensively in a narrow sector, thereby ignoring opportunities for profitable investment elsewhere. The theory can be translated into prosaic terms: "If a bulldozer costs $5,000 and shovels $2.50 each, if 1500 men can shovel in a day as much as one man can move with a bulldozer, and if manpower is abundant, capital can be saved by buying $3,750 worth of shovels, and disguised or open unemployment avoided."[2] This is a "static argument" and not very appealing to those interested in the "dynamics of growth."

A more "dynamic" argument advanced by some development theorists is that industries with high external economies are at the

[2] Charles P. Kindleberger, *Economic Development* (New York: McGraw-Hill Book Company, © 1958), p. 169. Used by permission.

same time frequently capital intensive. Such industries must be developed first in order to make profitable the allocation of investment resources to the labor-intensive industries for which the country presumably has an abundant factor endowment. Other theorists view this argument as a concession to those arguing for the adoption of techniques suitable to a country's factor endowment after subtracting those considerable lumps of capital needed for the overhead industries.

A close examination of the labor endowments of various under-developed countries, however, suggests that abundant labor does not necessarily mean inexpensive labor. Labor may indeed be lower in price than capital, but it may be even lower in efficiency and thus may be relatively more expensive than capital. Unedu-cated, industrially undisciplined, and undernourished labor, when coupled with artificial wage rigging and social security schemes, can prove to be expensive. Such a set of circumstances justifies the adoption of laborsaving and capital-intensive techniques, pro-vided, of course, that the skilled manpower is forthcoming to make production possible with the more capital-intensive techniques. In the absence of a supply of trained manpower the economy may be stuck on dead center with neither labor-intensive nor laborsaving techniques of production possible.

Disparity between the price of a factor and efficiency need not apply to labor only. Occasionally such disparity exists even for capital. Insofar as the capital market is imperfect, underpricing and overusing of capital can occur in a limited sector, making the capital unavailable in other sectors where it would earn a higher rate of return. The complaints of small business and agriculture in some countries with respect to access to capital markets indicate that such situations may not be too unusual.

Another factor influencing a country's choice of labor-intensive or capital-intensive techniques is the weight attached in its devel-opment program to the goals of maximum rate of increase in output and maximum employment. No problem exists when we are considering a case of constant returns to scale, with one output and two factors of production. Maximum output can be achieved by using capital in the way that employs most labor. On the other hand, the case of variable returns, with one output and two factors, introduces the possibility of conflict between the rate of increase in output and maximum unemployment. And the possibility of such conflict will almost surely increase in cases involving more than one output and economies of scale.

Charles P. Kindleberger summarizes the possibility of a conflict as follows:

Increasing returns to scale from capital investment which involves capital deepening puts the problem for a single output. In two or more industries, investment in one may give more income, in the other more employment. This may be true in each case, both directly and with external economies under which income and employment prospects created in other industries are imputed back to the original investment.[3]

He correctly indicates that in the final analysis it is not the economist who must make the choice between maximum output and maximum employment, though it should be the economist's duty to indicate how much of one must be given up for a fixed amount of the other.[4] Political considerations may dictate choosing maximum employment, especially when considerable unemployment exists, even though capital must still be used as efficiently as possible. On the other hand, if employment is a secondary consideration, a good case can be made for emphasizing the usual goal of economic development, which is the highest possible rate of increase in output.

THE ECONOMIC AND POLITICAL BASE FOR YUGOSLAVIA'S INDUSTRY

Our discussion of industrialization and economic development has in effect summarized the reasons for Yugoslavia's postwar

---

[3] Charles P. Kindleberger, *Economic Development* (New York: McGraw-Hill Book Company, © 1958) , p. 177. Used by permission.
[4] *Ibid.*

emphasis on industrialization. Yugoslavia shares with many other countries the view that industry is the key to further economic development. Unlike those of some other countries, however, Yugoslavia's views are to a great extent lodged in reality.

The country possesses unused and underutilized resources which are commonly thought to provide an industrial base.[5] A wide range of power sources such as water, coal, and petroleum exists in the country. Yugoslavia is second only to Norway in Europe in water-power potential. Although a large part, perhaps nine-tenths, of its coal resources is of low-calory lignite, modern utilization of this in thermal electric power plants and in semi-cooking is economically feasible. In 1960 with only 11–15 per cent of the prospective fields explored known reserves of industrial petroleum exceeded 21 million tons. The country also possesses the raw material base for a gas industry.

According to a very incomplete survey, it appears that other raw materials are available in sufficient quantity and quality to enable the country to support industry in something more than a hot-house. An adequate raw material base exists for nonferrous metallurgy. In reserves of zinc the country is fifteenth in the world, of copper ninth, of antimony eighth, of lead and bauxite seventh, and of mercury fifth. Conditions are also favorable for the production of sulphur, silver, gold, bismuth, cadmium, and silicon. Raw materials are insufficient to meet domestic requirements only in iron-alloy metals.

The available resources of iron ore have enabled the country to develop a modest iron and steel industry. Yugoslav iron ore is, however, below the world average in quality, so that the ore must be enriched. The ore which promises to aid the country to offset the poor quality of its iron is a nickel-bearing ore known as olitic. Although low in iron content, it is potentially important because of the quantity available, which is estimated at 500 million tons.

Virtually inexhaustible supplies are available of mineral earths

---

[5] For a summary of the country's raw material base, see Bogdan Djaković, *Yugoslavia's Non-ferrous Metals* (Belgrade: Kultura, 1958).

such as magnetite, heat-resisting clays, barites, chalk, gypsum, and quartz, and there are considerable supplies of bentonite, quartz sand, and rock salt. There are also veins of kaolin, infusorial earths, mica, and abrasives. Graphite sites have not yet been fully explored. Asbestos reserves are relatively small and low in quality. Ornamental stone of high quality is available in abundance in various sections of the country.

Although it has not been favored in the postwar period, agriculture is another important source of raw material for industry. Food-processing, tobacco, chemical, textile, paper, and leather industries are important outlets for agricultural products. In forest area and raw lumber output Yugoslavia is fourth in Europe, coming after Finland, Sweden, and France. These resources provide a basis for considerable woodworking and wood-processing industries.

In addition, it should be noted that Yugoslavia occupies a favorable geographic position. It is not only a maritime country, but it is linked to many central and east European countries by the Danube River. Rail and road links connect the country with other European countries, especially the other Balkans and through them with Asia Minor.

A large labor supply exists and will probably continue owing to the rather rapid population increase and the movement away from agriculture during the postwar period. Although labor is abundant, it is by no means inexpensive. Much of the available supply is inexperienced and industrially undisciplined, so that its efficiency is probably quite low. On the other hand, a favorable age structure, together with increasing investments in the human agent, suggests that this condition may be overcome before long.

More important perhaps is the existence in Yugoslavia of a tradition of "making money." Indeed, the Austrian War Council observed in 1699 that Serbs were "naturally born and trained" for trade.[6] So efficient were they, in fact, that German merchants could

---

[6] Traian Stoianovich, "Conquering Balkan Orthodox Merchant," *Journal of Economic History,* June 1960, p. 294.

not compete with them and insisted that various laws be enacted to curb Serbian economic activity.[7] By the end of the eighteenth century, as Traian Stoianovich writes:

Many immigrants from Old Serbia and Macedonia . . . had been merchants and artisans and were once well-to-do. In view of their numerous colonies and their settlement in compact groups in the towns of Hungary and both the towns and rural areas of Vojvodina, their family and business connections with the Ottoman Empire, and their repugnance for manual labor and the tilling of the soil, it was only logical that the Serbs of Hungary . . . should capture much of the Hungarian retail trade and an important segment of the foreign trade of Austria and Hungary with the Ottoman Empire.[8]

Serbian proclivities for "making money" were not limited to the Balkans and Central Europe but in fact extended into Russia and from Trieste, Rijeka (Fiume), and Dubrovnik to overseas areas including the Americas. One example will suffice to illustrate the point. A Hungarian Serb, Sava Tekelija, visiting the port of Odessa in Russia in 1811, observed in his autobiography: "I was amazed to hear mostly Serbian in the streets and coffee houses. Even the burgomaster was then Petrović, a Serb from Novi Sad. And there were many others. After the Serbian language, Italian was most audible; then Greek, Russian and Turkish. And there were many Jews." [9] If tradition is any criterion for the presence of entrepreneurship in a country, Yugoslavia appears to be well supplied. In fact, the Germans as recently as the last war complained that when Serbian prisoners of war began to arrive in Germany they brought the *pijaca* ("market") with them.

Whether or not this demonstrated entrepreneurship can find a constructive outlet within present-day Yugoslavia is another matter. Capital for industry is available through rigid domestic marshaling of available resources and from foreign loans and grants.

[7] *Ibid.,* pp. 294–95.
[8] *Ibid.,* pp. 265–66.
[9] Quoted, *ibid.,* p. 289.

Of course, capital is not the country's most abundant resource. Indeed, in the postwar period actual disinvestment in such critical sectors as agriculture, transport and communications, and housing has occurred occasionally in order to provide industry with capital.

Even if the economic base for industrialization was at best wobbly, strong political reasons would have impelled the country's leadership to undertake industrialization. Karl Marx and his followers did not envision the establishment of their society on a basically rural population. It was from an "industrial proletariat" that they expected support. Lacking such a "proletariat," the Marxist leadership in Yugoslavia apparently set about to create it through industrialization and at the expense, at first, of agriculture. Even though many of the farmers had initially supported the present leaders, the Marxists for theoretical reasons best understood by themselves viewed the farmers as a "politically unreliable group."

The rapid creation of an industrial proletariat involves attaching greater weight to the maximum rate of increase in industrial employment than to the maximum rate of output and hence to economic development. Under most cases of variable returns and more than one output these two goals may conflict. The rapid occupational change in favor of industry since the war suggests that considerable weight was attached to a rapid rate of increase in industrial employment. The conflict between this goal and that of output and economic development is indicated by the spotty performance of the economy until at least 1957, though other factors were probably equally important. In that year the desired balance between those employed in industry and those in agriculture began to be achieved, and the Yugoslav leadership apparently shifted emphasis to a general increase in output and development.

Data on structural changes in employment and on the rate of increase in national income are useful for the light that they shed on the economy's goals. It is estimated that between the early 1950's and 1957 or 1958 the country's industries absorbed three-fifths of the increase in the total labor force.[10] The nonagricultural population increased 18.5 per cent between 1945 and 1957, or at an average annual rate of 1.5 per cent, as compared to 3.9 per cent in the entire period from 1921 to 1938. The total agricultural population declined from a prewar figure of about 75 per cent to 60.9 per cent in 1953, 56 per cent in 1957, and 50 per cent in 1960. National income, on the other hand, increased at an average annual rate of about 2 per cent in the turbulent period 1948–52, rose to an average annual rate of 8 per cent in 1953–56, and then spurted forth to a 13 per cent annual rate in 1957–60. In the latter period a slight increase in the rate of unemployment occurred— from 2.7 per cent in 1956 to an average of 3.1 per cent in 1957–60. Labor productivity also increased from 2.2 per cent for the economy as a whole in 1954–56 to 6.9 per cent in 1957–60.

Another important political factor underlying the country's industrialization, the location in particular of its new postwar industries, and the choice of techniques has been the postwar conflict with the countries of Eastern Europe. Its changing political and economic status with respect to these countries has placed top priority on development and the location of industry in the interior away from the eastern frontiers. This has led to a relatively intensive development of industry in Bosnia and in effect disinvestment in such old industrial border areas as Vojvodina and Slavonia. Although the economic justification for the industrial development of these hard-to-reach areas may appear hazy, the strategic justifications are clear-cut. Fortunately for the economic side of the argument, many of the areas that were the beneficiaries of this development are also areas where considerable raw materials exist.

This does not mean, of course, that before 1957 the capital-intensive techniques and industries were disregarded. Quite the contrary. In the Key Industry Investment Program around 1948 considerable emphasis was placed on such overhead industries as those developing hydroelectric power and other energy sources.

[10] G. W. Hoffman and F. W. Neal, *Yugoslavia and the New Communism* (New York: Twentieth Century Fund, 1962), p. 322.

At the same time substantial resources were devoted, for example, to the building of a machine tool industry, which is not, strictly speaking, an overhead industry. The Yugoslavs, however, did not place as much emphasis on the development of heavy industry as did the Soviets.

RESULTS AND PROBLEMS

In order to bring the postwar development of industry into proper perspective it is useful to summarize its development in the interwar period. Although slowed down during the depression years, industry did develop to a considerable extent. The machine-building, textile, food-processing, timber, chemical, and nonmetallic industries moved ahead. With respect to the rated power of machinery, however, the situation left much to be desired. Of the total rated capacity over 60 per cent was lodged in electric power stations. In no other single branch of industry was there a substantial employment of machine power. In only one branch and that chemicals was there anything approaching a pattern of capital-intensive growth. The low capital-labor ratio that prevailed reflected the scarcity of capital, the relative abundance of labor, and the small size of the units involved.[11]

The number of factories increased by 113 per cent, at rated capacity potential employment increased by 89 per cent, and rated capacity increased by 52 per cent in the interwar period.[12] No more than one-quarter of the population increase of 3 million could have been absorbed in industry. The economy as a whole and industry in particular suffered from a lack of capital and an up-to-date technology, a low level of skills in the population, and internal and external conditions generally unfavorable to development brought about for the most part by the economic depression of the 30's.

In any appraisal of the country's postwar industrial output considerable caution should be exercised in using the available

[11] B. Ward, "Yugoslavia," in *Economic Development,* ed. by A. Pepelasis, L. Mears, and I. Adelman (New York: Harper and Brothers, 1961) , p. 535.
[12] *Ibid.*

data. This is particularly true if attempts are made at international comparisons. According to the Federal Statistical Institute, "industrial output" is defined so as to include manufacturing, mining, and quarrying in their specific senses. It includes the production of electric energy, mining, and the processing of mine, forest, and agricultural raw materials. Excluded from industrial output are arts and crafts and construction. The monthly reports on which estimates of industrial output are based approximate something over 90 per cent of the country's manufacturing, mining, and quarrying output. The data thus do not include all manufacturing enterprises and thereby underestimate the country's output.

Yugoslav nomenclature does not conform to the International Standard Classification of Economic Activities. Available data are based on the nomenclature of activities compiled by the Federal Planning Committee in 1947 and classified into twenty branches plus one branch called "Other Miscellaneous Manufacturing Activities." The latter contains those enterprises which could not be classified under the official twenty and includes such manufactured articles as plastics, sports equipment, buttons, musical instruments, and toys.

The preparation of the country's index of the physical values of industrial production merits comment. According to the methodological explanation, monthly and annual data on finished production classified according to the above nomenclature are used. The weights are derived from income originating in the process of production within, and depreciation charges of, enterprises. The weighting system has, however, undergone frequent change. The data for 1951 were used in those indexes relating to 1939 and 1946–53. In 1953 new weights were obtained and the indexes for these years corrected. The series of indexes thus computed were linked without correction for the various changes in weighting. The net result is that a very hazy picture is obtained of the country's over-all postwar industrial output. And as noted by the Federal Statistical Institute, this is particularly true if attempts are made to estimate, for example, labor productivity in the various branches of manufacturing.

Table 29 presents available data on industrial expansion in 1960 relative to 1939 and 1952. To judge from these data, the most notable expansion occurred in the production of electrical equipment, petroleum, metal manufactures, chemicals, iron, and steel. (For the most part these industries are very capital intensive.)

TABLE 29. Volume of production in 1960

| | 1960 production compared with | |
Industry and Mining	1939 = 100	1952 = 100
Electricity	752	327
Coal	264	184
Petroleum	1,835	435
Iron and steel	686	391
Nonferrous metallurgy	299	206
Production and processing of other ores	450	260
Metal manufactures	862	328
Electrical equipment	5,000	622
Chemicals	745	455
Building materials	393	222
Wood products	256	208
Paper	433	261
Textiles	267	223
Leather and footwear	308	241
Rubber	463	277
Food	363	319
Tobacco	177	141

Source: "Industrial Expansion and Its Results," *Yugoslav Survey*, March 1961, p. 884.

These branches of industry are almost all postwar developments in that their prewar production was modest. A more accurate picture is perhaps provided by per capita industrial production of selected items presented in Table 30. These figures suggest that industrial output is still relatively modest in comparison to that of most other European countries.

Much of the industrialization effort in the period 1948–55 has gone into the construction and expansion of existing facilities. The most notable examples are the iron and steel works at Zenica, Sisak, and Nikšić, the Ivo Lola Ribar machine tool complex at Zeleznik, the heavy machinery works at Listostroj in Ljubljana, the automobile plant at Maribor, the electrical equipment works

TABLE 30. Per capita industrial production of selected items for 1939 and 1957–62

Item	1939	1957	1958	1959	1960	1961	1962
Electric energy, K.W.H.	72	342	404	445	485	533	598
Coal, kg.	432	987	1,044	1,159	1,234	1,294	1,311
Crude oil, kg.	0	22	25	33	51	72	81
Crude oil processing, kg.	6	57	61	65	70	73	88
Crude steel, kg.	14	58	62	71	78	82	85
Cement, kg.	55	109	108	122	130	126	134
Sulphuric acid, kg.	1.4	6.8	6.9	7.0	7.1	13.7	15.2
Soap, kg.	0.8	1.8	1.6	2.7	2.8	2.9	3.1
Paper and cardboard, kg.	2.6	6.7	7.1	7.6	8.5	10.7	12.3
Cotton fabrics, sq. m.	7	11	12	13	14	14	16
Woolen fabrics, sq. m.	0.8	1.8	1.8	2.1	2.5	2.3	2.3
Socks and stockings, pair	1.4	1.8	1.8	2.0	2.3	2.2	2.2
Footwear, pair	0.6	1.1	1.3	1.4	1.6	1.7	1.7
Edible oil, kg.	1.3	1.8	2.3	2.5	2.8	3.0	3.9
Cans, kg.	0.3	2.0	2.1	2.7	3.7	3.9	4.3
Sugar, kg.	7	12	10	13	14	12	12
Beer, liter	3	6	7	7	9	10	9

Source: Federal Statistical Institute, *Statistical Pocket-Book of Yugoslavia* (Belgrade: The Institute, 1961 and 1963), pp. 50 (1961), 55 (1963).

of Rade Končar in Zagreb, the Sevojno copper-rolling works, the Svetozarevo cable works, and the Jugovinil plastics plant in Split. Even the food-processing industry came in for large-scale expansion.

A study of the distribution of Yugoslav enterprises by number of employees, total fixed capital, and total net product indicates that relatively small enterprises are not dominant in the country's socialized sector of production. As indicated in Table 31, capital, output, and employment are concentrated in a relatively few enterprises. Thus in 1958 213 enterprises with over 1,000 employees accounted for 46 per cent of the total industrial employment, 52 per cent of the fixed capital, and 53 per cent of the net product.

In 1958 a typical enterprise (outside handicrafts) employed an

TABLE 31. Number of employees, fixed capital, and net product by groups of enterprises in 1958

Number of employees	Number of enterprises	Total number of employees	Fixed capital in millions of dinars	Net product in millions of dinars
1–15	139	1,487	7,144	713
16–29	183	4,114	9,648	2,175
30–60	347	15,581	63,905	9,929
61–125	552	49,777	112,971	30,406
126–250	551	99,217	225,460	60,188
251–500	459	163,134	257,853	110,113
501–1,000	266	190,811	316,406	173,218
1001–2,000	139	190,933	439,953	212,959
Over 2,000	74	261,025	667,675	217,719
Total *	2,710	976,079	2,111,015	817,421

Source: Research Department, National Bank of Yugoslavia.
* Excludes handicrafts in the social and private sectors.

average of about 200 people and had 390 million dinars of fixed capital and an annual output of about 130 million dinars. Handicraft enterprises totaling 3,781 in the socialized sector of the economy accounted for 120,560 employees. Figures for the private sector are not available for 1958. The census of December 1959, however, indicates that there were 116,000 such workshops with a total employment of 150,000. Unlike the shops in the socialized sector, they are prevented by law from employing more than five persons. In addition, they were subject in the past to a heavy tax of up to 75 per cent of their total income. A later chapter will discuss new measures designed to deal with the private sector.

The large number of private handicraft establishments suggests the government's lack of interest in developing small industrial enterprises. These handicraft establishments supplement in part the production of larger enterprises in the socialized sector. They do service and repair work chiefly, one of the most underdeveloped areas of the country's economy. Although a majority of these private craftsmen barely manage to scratch out a living, some do quite well for themselves. To reduce the growing tendency of private craftsmen to go into production on their own, the government apparently intends to tighten enforcement of regulations and collection of taxes as well as to increase repair facilities in the socialized sector.

Lack of balance between small and large establishments has not been the only problem to plague industry. Insufficient stocks of raw materials together with problems of obtaining working capital have placed a drag on industry and the economy as a whole. These factors were recognized, and after 1957 more emphasis was placed on providing the economy with increased working capital and in permitting enterprises a greater freedom of action.

In view of the continuing investment in expansion of industrial capacity, perhaps the most important problems are those arising out of the insufficient utilization of existing capacity.[13] In 1956, for example, it is estimated that the degree of utilization of industrial capacity was about 77 per cent, and the volume of inactive fixed assets amounted to 400 billion dinars, or about 20 per cent of the total invested resources in the same year.[14] Such underutilization is particularly serious in some of the most modern plants. As noted elsewhere in this study, poor organization, unrealistic output

[13] Two issues of *Ekonomski pregled* ("Economic Survey"; nos. 2 and 3, 1960) are devoted to an examination of the problems arising out of the country's industrialization efforts.

[14] N. Čobeljić, *Politika i metodi privrednog razvoja Jugoslavije 1947–56* ("Policy and Methods of Economic Development in Yugoslavia 1947–56"; Belgrade: Nolit, 1959), pp. 197–370.

norms, inferior quality and assortment of products, high prices, and an inadequate number of qualified personnel are the principal reasons given by Yugoslavs for the underutilization of existing capacity. The analysis in Chapter 7 suggests that still another and perhaps more important reason is the system of worker-management.

The country's experience is interesting in the light that it sheds on the problems of labor-intensive and capital-intensive techniques as well as on the issue of borrowed technology. All other things being equal, a good case could be made for adopting labor-intensive techniques as suited to the country. Interwar experience suggests that such techniques have in fact met with a measure of success. But all other things, however, are not equal. In the first place, the application of such techniques in the prewar period, according to influential Yugoslav opinion, did not bring about a sufficiently rapid rate of development. In the second place, and as we already noted, the country's most abundant factor is not necessarily its cheapest factor. Indeed, it is almost a national joke that in order to supplement their incomes farmers seek employment in industry, preferably on the third shift (11 P.M. to 7 A.M.) in order to be paid while they "sleep" following a day's work on their farms.

The shift in emphasis to more capital-intensive techniques and the drive for increased efficiency may at first appear to be incorrectly dated as "since 1957." In a sense this is true because heavy investment in industry has occurred throughout the postwar period, and in most of these industries capital-intensive techniques are applied. Probably the most important factor contributing to the choice of such techniques is the operation of the worker-management system with its built-in bias for capital-intensive techniques. The Yugoslavs have in fact allocated their capital to the purchase of steam shovels rather than hand shovels. They have, however, added an interesting refinement to this allocation by calling in their abundant factor to stand around and watch. Since 1957, however, the watchers have not received the same welcome as before. In the first five months of 1962, 175 enterprises in Serbia reported a labor surplus of 12,500 workers. Over 58 per cent of those subsequently laid off were nonskilled.[15]

The Yugoslav decision to adopt the most up-to-date technology with its large capital requirements can also be considered as something out of the Schumpeterian world but in different form. The socialist sector of industry has been assigned the role of entrepreneur in the sense that it is the innovator which undertakes new combinations of the factors of production, whereas the other sectors of the economy have more or less been assigned the role of ordinary managerial activity. The latter sectors, especially the private sectors of agriculture and craftsmen, concern themselves with directing production under existing techniques while industry concerns itself with something new.

Unlike the more traditional view of the economic world, the Schumpeterian view as seen through Yugoslav glasses involves a considerable degree of uncertainty and risk, so that development does not take place gradually and smoothly. Under these circumstances investment cannot be based on rational calculations, and the usual emphasis placed upon the act of harboring resources in the development process is overstressed. Industry in its entrepreneurial role must be permitted to "raid society's circular flow" if it is to obtain the resources necessary to carry out innovations whose fruits will then raise all sectors of the economy to an ever higher level of development.

If this analysis is correct, and there is little reason to believe it is not, it helps to explain why industry has been given such favorable treatment in the postwar period. Undoubtedly empirical evidence also influenced Yugoslav decisions on industry. Past experience in some other European countries suggests that the most rapid development did in fact take place in those countries that applied the most up-to-date technology in their industries. Moreover, no less a person than Veblen stressed the important role that the most modern borrowed technology plays in a country undertaking industrialization.

[15] *Politika* (Belgrade) , Aug. 31, 1962, p. 6.

Yugoslavia's foreign exchange system has also contributed to the choice of techniques. An unrealistic and overvalued exchange rate may actually make foreign capital equipment appear cheap. This is probably an important factor contributing to the establishment in Yugoslavia of so-called screw-driver factories. Such factories operate on foreign equipment and product parts, hence the name screw-driver factories. The most notable of these appear to be some of the plants engaged in producing television sets, refrigerators, and automobiles. Insofar as the labor costs of assembly in Yugoslavia are low, there is some justication in undertaking such operations, though the costs and benefits to the economy would be difficult to evaluate.

12.▲

AGRICULTURE

TOP PRIORITY TO INDUSTRY OR AGRICULTURE?

One of the most heated and crucial issues in economic development is whether industry or agriculture is to be favored in a country's development schemes. The previous chapter has examined some of the arguments advanced in favor of industrialization. All too often such arguments are based on the superficial argument that industrial countries are developed and rich and agricultural countries underdeveloped and poor. A symptom of development is taken as its cause. The industrialization accompanied by increased consumption is a different animal from the industrialization forced by government largely at the expense of consumption.

Economic arguments in favor of such industrialization are indeed weak. Particularly notorious is the argument that in underdeveloped areas the marginal product of labor in agriculture is close to zero if indeed it is not zero. The country's agricultural output would therefore not be altered if such surplus labor were transferred to the industry created by government. It does not follow, of course, that a country should undertake forced industrialization even if the marginal product of labor in agriculture is zero, since it may very well be increased by increasing the capital employed in agriculture or indeed by reorganizing agriculture. There is also a tendency to neglect the costs of urbanization that must surely be incurred as a consequence of the transfer of people out of agriculture. More important is the fact that the supporters of this view have been tardy in presenting empirical evidence to substantiate their argument. In fact, available evidence suggests that agricultural labor's marginal product may well be significantly above zero.[1]

Matters of expediency, political dogma, and a penchant for the spectacular appear to be the motivating forces underlying governmental prejudice against agriculture and for compulsory industrialization. It is more expedient to favor industry than to attempt to persuade the poor and largely illiterate farmers of many underdeveloped countries to forsake their traditional way of doing things. In industry workers will start from the beginning. It is political dogma in some countries because their "scriptures" call for the creation of an industrial proletariat. And, finally, it is more spectacular to have a steel mill than to spread limited resources over the countryside.

This does not mean that agriculture has been everywhere and always snubbed. Indeed, various Communist countries have attempted to mechanize crops and in some countries have completely revolutionized the economic and social organization of the countryside. By and large these efforts have failed to produce the desired results. In the United States considerable resources are devoted to improvement and expansion of the agricultural output. To judge from the stock piles of various commodities together with the price-rigging schemes current in the United States, American efforts have been too successful, suggesting that too much has been given to the agricultural sector.

If an underdeveloped country desires to achieve balanced economic development, then, all other things being equal, a strong case can be made for granting agriculture access to investment funds. A common characteristic of such countries is a relatively high income elasticity of demand for food and a relatively low income elasticity of demand for products of industry. Large-scale investment programs that allocate resources with little heed to

---

[1] See T. W. Schultz, "Latin-American Economic Policy Lessons," *American Economic Review Papers and Proceedings*, May 1956.

these elasticities may introduce severe distortions into the economy and seriously overburden it.

An illustration may explain the problem. Suppose an underdeveloped country allocates considerable investment to industry at the expense, say, of agriculture. The net effect is to reduce the supply of agricultural products at the very time when demand for these products increases. Contrariwise, the output of industrial products with relatively low income elasticities of demand increases. The prices of agricultural products will rise relative to those for industrial products.

One way to preserve balanced development without at the same time allocating additional resources to agriculture is to import food and export industrial products. In this way the terms of trade between agricultural and industrial sectors can be held in balance. Great Britain, for example, adopted such a solution in the nineteenth century when it turned to international trade as a means of preserving a balance between agriculture and industry.

In relatively closed economies such an alternative is not available. The rise in food prices may not result in an increase in the output of agricultural products, and the decline in the prices of domestic industrial products may not induce people to purchase much more of the latter. Such an economy may be well advised to preserve a balance between the two sectors via an investment policy that enables agriculture to increase output and so keep pace with that of the industrial sector, thereby steadying the terms of trade between these two sectors. In fact, however, all countries are open economies in the sense that they engage in some trade with other countries.

Thus far the analysis has implicitly assumed that consumption paths are fixed as income increases, so that changes in the terms of trade between the agricultural and industrial sectors change neither the patterns of consumption nor the allocation of resources from the supply side. Such an assumption implies, in effect, that price elasticities are zero or close to it. Many people argue, especially those advocating planning, that this is in fact the case in underdeveloped economies. If so, it would appear best to balance output between the various sectors on the basis of information provided by income elasticities instead of relying on present prices. These prices are inadequate indicators of prospective prices because they do not sufficiently reflect demand-and-supply changes occurring as a result of changing conditions underlying demand and supply.

When, however, price elasticities are not low, so that there is responsiveness to price changes, any diversion in the composition of output increases from that called for by income elasticities of demand will be offset by changes in consumption and output brought about by the price system. It is possible, consequently, to allocate investment, not on the basis of sectoral balance, but rather on the marginal efficiency of capital in various uses regardless of the sector. And the criterion for investment should be the projects with the highest marginal efficiency of capital. Under these circumstances the argument for balance per se between agriculture and industry loses much of its force. Indeed, if the price system works at all, investment should be free to flow into the most profitable areas of the economy. Such adjustments as are required can be undertaken by the economy itself instead of trusting these adjustments to a bureaucratic planning body.

Very few underdeveloped countries and their governments have an inclination or a desire to promote balanced economic development. For reasons already discussed many of these countries insist on identifying economic development with industrialization. It is ironic, however, that their desires for industrialization can frequently be more readily fulfilled by promoting agriculture.

How can this be? Consider, first, a closed economy and the so-called complex elasticity case in which negative price elasticities exist for both the output of agriculture and industry.[2] Suppose also that as real incomes rise, the urban and rural population's demand for agricultural products increases less than proportionately. Suppose further that in the region of equilibrium, agricultural households consume more of their own output if prices rise relative to those for industrial products. This is simply another way of stating

[2] Stephen Enke, *Economics for Development* (Englewood, N. J.: Prentice-Hall, 1963), pp. 547–52.

the common observation that in many underdeveloped countries agricultural households take more of their income in food as their incomes grow than do urban dwellers or even agricultural households in more advanced countries.

Under these circumstances a general increase in agricultural productivity per worker will result in a proportionately greater decrease in the price of the agricultural output. The urban-industrial population will find that its income in terms of agricultural goods has increased by something more than the increase in agricultural output. In effect, agricultural prices will fall proportionately more than the increase in output as the rural population attempts to sell the extra output rather than consume it. As a result, real earnings will become comparatively smaller in agriculture than in industry; hence there may be an outflow of labor from agriculture into industry.

Thus, a low income elasticity of demand for agricultural output and an even lower price elasticity for such products when combined with increased productivity in agriculture will expel resources from this sector. This conclusion is not contradicted when, as in most underdeveloped countries, the income elasticity of demand for agricultural products is still comparatively high. It simply means that considerably greater productivity in agriculture is necessary to shift resources into industry.

In the more general case, however, the conclusions are not so clear. An increase in agricultural productivity may simply increase exports. This does not mean that the country will not benefit from such trade. It does mean that in the first approximation economic development defined as synonymous with industrialization will not occur as a result of increasing agricultural productivity. But secondary and tertiary effects of such expanded international trade may well promote industrialization by increasing the resources at the country's disposal.

PREWAR AGRICULTURAL CONDITIONS IN YUGOSLAVIA

Before World War II 75 per cent of the country's population or 11,600,000 people were engaged in agriculture. The agricultural population had increased between World Wars I and II so that by the 1930's there were 1.14 agricultural inhabitants for each hectare of arable land.[3] This was three times the density of the more advanced European countries.

The pressure on the land was intensified by the primitive methods of farming. To judge from the studies of Jordan Blazevski *et al.*, approximately 75 per cent of the plows in use were made of wood; 17 per cent of all agricultural landholdings were less than two hectares, and more than one-third of the agricultural population possessed such small holdings. The productivity of labor engaged in agriculture left much to be desired. In the period between 1929 and 1939 agricultural output increased about 12 per cent, while labor engaged in this sector increased by over 10 per cent. If these figures are correct, they suggest a very modest gain indeed in agricultural productivity. The terms of trade in the years between 1923 and 1939 turned against agriculture in favor of industrial products by over 20 per cent. The result was that the incomes of those engaged in agriculture were among the lowest in Europe.

By 1932 every third farm was seriously in debt. Indeed, in that year farm debt amounted to about 7 billion dinars and farmers paid over 1 billion dinars annually in interest. Farm income on the other hand amounted to only 7 billion dinars. These factors combined to give the individual farmer a rather grim standard of living. Corn was the basic diet. Meat and sugar were rare treats. Tobacco, salt, matches, and petrol—articles sold under government monopoly conditions, the proceeds being the principal source of government revenue—were comparatively expensive. Rural households made their own clothing and footwear, thereby excluding such households further from the market. Malnutrition in the country was more a rule than an exception, so that individual productivity suffered further. Health facilities available to

[3] Berislav Šefer, "Standard of Living of Agricultural Producers in Yugoslavia, in *Transformation of Yugoslav Agriculture*, ed. by Jordan Blazevski, Vladimir Stipetić, and Miodrag Jevremović (Belgrade: Beogradski Grafički Zavod [Belgrade's Graphic Institute], 1951), p. 93. See also S. D. Agoroff, Jenö Vegh, and Alexander D. Bilimovich, *The Agricultural Economy of the Danubian Countries, 1935–45* (Stanford: Stanford University Press, 1955).

the rural population were practically nonexistent. More than half of the rural population were illiterate and indeed in such areas as the Kosmet, Macedonia, Bosnia, and Hercegovina the illiteracy rate was as high as 85 per cent. Hence one important means for spreading knowledge about new techniques for increasing productivity was useless. As for the purchase of industrial products by the agrarian population, this was almost nonexistent, suggesting among other things a high income elasticity of demand for food whose effect tended to inhibit the development of industry and thus reduce alternative sources of employment. Unemployment ranged from 6 to 8 per cent in the interwar period, and sometimes, as in the 1930's, as high as 20 per cent.

In fairness to the prewar government it should be noted that many sources of the country's troubles were beyond its reach. Two of these sources were of particular importance. One, of course, was the world-wide depression of the 1930's, which struck Yugoslavia with particular severity. The other was its external trade, which was dominated by Germany. These two sources combined to create for the country's economy, and agriculture in particular, extremely difficult problems.

The Yugoslav government attempted to combat the domestic effects of the depression by various countercyclical measures including public works. Its efforts were futile and the economy slipped from bad to worse. Yugoslavia simply did not have the resources or the time to grapple with all its manifold problems before being plunged into World War II.

All other things being equal, Yugoslavia's economic difficulties could have been mitigated if not solved through the expansion of its external trade, an expansion which occurred from the mid-1930's until 1941. The additional resources thus acquired could have gone into increasing the productivity of agriculture, which if it did not promote industrialization per se would at least have increased the well-being of its citizens.

Unfortunately all other things were not equal, and instead of promoting the well-being of the citizens the expanded foreign trade ironically helped to finance their destruction in World War

II. Yugoslavia's increased exports in the late 1930's were primarily to Germany. A favorable balance of trade existed with Germany owing to the ready market in that country for Yugoslavia's agricultural products and other raw materials. Exports always exceeded imports in this period, and under normal circumstances Yugoslavia could have obtained from the surpluses so generated the badly needed resources for its internal development.

The Germans, however, impounded the fruits of Yugoslav labor in a special clearings fund under German control. A stated percentage (larger than the amount normally spent) was required to be spent for German goods. Part of the sales in Germany might be used by Yugoslavia to buy goods in third countries. But this use of German funds (essentially the triangular use of funds that Germany acquired by exporting more than she imported in trade with third countries) was strictly limited. Yugoslavia's dependence on the German export market in effect forced it to lend to Germany desperately needed resources.

For their troubles in promoting international trade the Yugoslavs received from Germany occasional trainloads of Bayer Aspirin and harmonicas and in 1941–45 a disastrous visit from the German Army, whose development their meager resources helped finance. The visit by the German Army and its debased band of camp followers dealt an almost irreparable blow to the Yugoslav countryside. According to official estimates, Yugoslavia lost 61.6 per cent of its horses, 55.6 per cent of its cattle, 63.3 per cent of its sheep and goats, 58.7 per cent of its pigs, 29.2 per cent of its orchards, over 50 per cent of its plows, 62 per cent of the farmers' carts, and 50 per cent of the tractors.[4] To this may be added the melancholy statistic of 1,700,000 people, or 10 per cent of the population, killed, and most of these people were engaged in agriculture. Yet Germans (both East and West) are still strangely silent about settling their proper share of this rather remarkable bill.

As though to counter the argument that history never repeats

[4] Dimitrije Bajalica, "Agricultural Cooperatives," in *Transformation of Yugoslav Agriculture*, p. 38.

itself, the Soviet Union in the immediate postwar period attempted to repeat the successful German experiment with Yugoslavia. Fortunately for the Yugoslavs, they were not caught a second time—at least not as disastrously. Indeed, the postwar "brotherly" Soviet squeeze has left the Yugoslavs wary of further international embraces. Recent American attempts to exclude Yugoslavia from most favored nation treatment in international trade have not exactly eased Yugoslav fears on this score. This does not mean that the Yugoslavs are now searching for solutions to their problems by autarchy. It does mean that the tasks of the country's postwar government are just as formidable as those of the government in the interwar period. And in no other sector is this better illustrated than in agriculture.

REORGANIZING AGRICULTURE IN THE POSTWAR PERIOD

A review of postwar attempts to come to grips with the problems of agriculture as these problems are viewed by the government is helpful to an understanding of the wider problems that plague the country's economy. The new postwar government attempted to generate "popular support" for itself through several measures designed to influence agriculture. In August 1945 the first postwar Land Reform Act was passed. The act was drafted on the principle that the "land belongs to those that till it." Under its provisions the holdings of private individuals were limited to 25 to 35 hectares. The reform affected 161,171 holdings comprising about 1,566,000 hectares of land. Landholdings of banks and industrial firms, together with all the equipment on the land, were expropriated by the government without compensation. Church organizations were limited to 10 hectares in the case of properties having historical value and up to 30 hectares of cultivable land in addition to 30 hectares of forest land.

Individuals who left their lands and did not return to them before January 5, 1948, lost them without compensation. These individuals comprised a large part of the country's prewar German minority, many of whom severely compromised themselves during the war and subsequently fled the country. Recent census estimates indicate, however, that 40,000 Germans still live in the country and enjoy Yugoslav citizenship. Needless to say, these individuals were not involved in the activities of the German Army of occupation or in those of its camp followers.

The Second Land Reform Act was passed in 1953. Under its provisions private holdings were limited to 10 or 15 hectares, depending on the fertility of the soil. Over 66,000 private holders lost 275,900 hectares of land. Such owners were compensated at the rate of 100 to 300 U. S. dollars per hectare for their losses. In contrast to the first land reform this second postwar reform did not distribute the acquired lands to private individuals but rather allocated them to farms in the socialist sector of the economy.

The second land reform followed on the heels of the 1948–52 attempts to force individual farmers into the Soviet type of kolkhoz collectives. Political dogma overcame economics. Attempts to prove that the Yugoslav Communists were better Marxists than their Soviet counterparts provided impetus to the collectivization drive. Economics entered into the picture ostensibly via a desire to reap the benefits of large-scale production. The result, however, was a resounding failure, both politically and economically.

It became painfully obvious to many people that one hundred poor farm families forced into one vast kolkhoz, or peasant work cooperative as it is called in Yugoslavia, did not by that fact alone produce one prosperous farm. Yugoslav experience suggests that simple changes in property rights and boundaries together with a shifting of the rural population do not always result in any spectacular increase in farm output. Indeed, the collectivization effort produced serious internal political repercussions. The vast majority of individual farmers, particularly those who were somewhat better off than the average, were unwilling to enter into such arrangements voluntarily. Force was required and its application very nearly resulted in an internal political upheaval. The lack of popularity of the peasant work cooperative is indicated by the rapid withdrawal from these organizations when membership became voluntary following the 1953 reforms. In 1959 there were only 229 of these cooperatives with 24,580 members working on 1.2 per cent of the country's total agricultural area.[5]

Also important in the socialist sector of agriculture are the state-owned farms and the holdings of state agricultural institutes operated under direct government supervision and control. In 1959 these organizations held approximately 5 per cent of the total agricultural area.

Since most agricultural land is privately owned, it is important to consider what the government is doing to aid the private agricultural sector. One type of organization that has achieved some success in coming to grips with the problem of agricultural output has been the general purpose agricultural cooperative. These cooperatives are formed on the basis of voluntary association of individual farmers who maintain titles to their land. Such an organization is not new. It was popular in the country in the interwar period, perhaps because of the poverty of the soil. Indeed in 1939 there were 10,628 agricultural cooperatives with a membership of over 1.3 million.[6] In 1957–58 over 1 million hectares of private land were represented in the general purpose agricultural cooperatives, and this figure has been constantly growing. It should be noted, however, that the present cooperatives differ from the prewar organizations in that they are not, strictly speaking, an association of private landowners; rather they serve as a "mechanism for integrating the socialist and private sectors of agriculture."

These cooperatives are managed directly by their members. The management bodies and officers consist of the assembly, the cooperative council, the executive board, and the director. The assembly, consisting of all the members of the cooperative, establishes the rules under which the organization operates, adopts the prospective plan of development, and solves other basic problems involved in the operation of the cooperative. The cooperative

[5] George W. Hoffman and Fred W. Neal, *Yugoslavia and the New Communism* (New York: Twentieth Century Fund, 1962), p. 266.

[6] *Ibid.*, p. 269.

council, consisting of 30 to 80 members, concerns itself with the annual plan and such other problems as fixing the permissible level of debt of the individual producing components of the cooperative. It also elects the members of the executive board. The executive board, consisting of 5 to 11 members, ensures the implementation of the cooperative's plan and also watches over the cooperative's funds. The director, who is appointed by the municipal people's committee, is the chief executive of the cooperative and is responsible for the day-to-day operations of the organization.

Socialist cooperation, as that term is understood by Yugoslav theoreticians and applied to agriculture, means any form of productive cooperation between socialist economic organizations and private individual farms. This cooperation takes various forms such as purchase and sale agreements, technical assistance and services, the granting of production loans, the extension of mechanized cultivation to private farmers for a price, and cooperation in production between the private farmer and the cooperative whereby the two as joint owners of the final output share in the proceeds either according to an agreed-upon contract or under a somewhat similar arrangement in which the cooperative is the owner of the final product and pays the private farmer a fixed price for the use of his resources.

These are the alternatives open to the private farmer for improving his position. He, of course, has the additional alternative of not cooperating with the socialist sector; he then is thrown on his own meager resources. Cooperation between the private farmer and the socialist sector has been growing. One reason for the increase in such cooperation is that the crop yields on farms cooperating with the socialist sector have been larger on the average than those on private farms divorced from such cooperation. In addition, the ready availability of credit to individuals cooperating has been an added inducement to the private farmer to enter into arrangements with the socialist sector.

Although these arrangements give the appearance of monopsony, it would be erroneous to conclude that the chief beneficiary of such cooperation is always the cooperatives. The insistence on the part of some agricultural cooperatives on cooperation at any price has often resulted in singular losses to the cooperatives. This may be attributed to the inability of some of the cooperatives to grasp the significance of the problems that face the individual farmers and the country's agriculture. At times individual farmers have taken advantage of the cooperative by insisting on short-term contracts, when long-term contracts are more in the interest of the cooperatives. Some of the cooperatives have mounted a virtual political campaign to obtain cooperation from individual farmers. Once such cooperation was obtained, they were unable to fulfill their promises. The result has been increased skepticism on the part of private farmers.

Economists and others have continually warned the cooperatives that the initiative toward cooperation must come from individual farmers; otherwise the entire program may fail. The individual must be convinced that cooperation does in fact offer him an opportunity to raise his standard of living by increasing his productivity. Some economists argue, moreover, that there is no point in pushing such cooperation since it ultimately depends upon the resources at the disposal of the cooperative. And these resources at the current stage of the economy's development are not large.

PROBLEMS AND PROSPECTS

Some idea of the problems confronting the country's agriculture, and indeed the economy in general, is obtained from estimates of the income elasticities of demand for food. Table 32 summarizes the estimates given by Vladimir Stipetić in his study of agricultural income elasticities for food in Yugoslavia.[7]

[7] "Razmatranja o jugoslovenskom tržištu prehambrenih proizvoda u razdoblju 1956–61 godine" ("Observations on the Yugoslav Market for Food Products in the Period 1956–61"), *Ekonomski pregled* ("Economic Survey"), no. 10–11 (1962), pp. 801–34.

TABLE 32. Income elasticities of demand for food for four-member urban households and agricultural households for 1957

Category	Four-member urban household	Agricultural household
All food	0.585	0.859
Meat and fish	1.020	N.A.
Fats	0.238	N.A.
Milk, milk products & eggs	1.015	N.A.
Fruit	1.131	N.A.

Source: Vladimir Stipetić, "Razmatranja o jugoslovenskom tržištu prehambrenih proizvoda u razdoblju 1956–61 godine" ("Observations on the Yugoslav Market for Food Products in the Period 1956–61"), *Ekonomski pregled* ("Economic Survey"), no. 10–11 (1962), p. 819.
N.A. = not available.

These income elasticity estimates are derived from a cross section of family budget data for 1958.[8] The average income elasticity of the demand for food in the country is reported by Stipetić to be 0.634 for 1956–61. Insofar as I have been able to determine, the concepts of "income" and "food" used in these studies are comparable to those used by various international agencies for similar studies (e.g., the FAO's *The State of Food and Agriculture in 1957* published in Rome in 1959).

What these estimates suggest is that Yugoslavia, if judged by the average income elasticity of demand for food of 0.634, can be typed (using T. W. Schultz's classification of income elasticities for food between 0.75 and 0.25) as an "intermediate food drain" community.[9] In effect, the country is in a transitional demographic stage in which population growth is not altogether independent of food supplies. This classification also suggests that Yugoslavs are experiencing a gradual rise in their standard of living. Though not strictly comparable it is of interest to note that income elasticity estimates for the United States in the late 1940's were roughly

[8] For various problems arising out of the construction and use of income elasticity estimates for food, see T. W. Schultz, *The Economic Organization of Agriculture* (New York: McGraw-Hill, 1953), pp. 44–82.

[9] *Ibid.*, p. 32.

below 0.30 and for American urban dwellers in 1918 approximately 0.57.[10]

A very different story unfolds, however, when an account is taken of conditions in the countryside. To judge from the estimates above the income elasticity of demand for food by agricultural households is 0.859. Such an estimate would place the Yugoslav countryside about on a par with India.[11] According to Schultz's terminology, the countryside can be characterized as a "high food drain" area where 75 per cent (income elasticity 0.75 or greater) or more of the population's income is used normally to acquire food. This is basically the situation covered by the Ricardo-Malthus-Mill formulation and sometimes referred to as the preindustrial demographic class.[12]

The comparatively high income elasticity of demand for food in agricultural households (0.859) is apparently for home-produced farm products. If so, it suggests a "backward sloping supply schedule" for home-produced farm products. When the terms of trade turn in favor of agriculture, the agricultural household sells less food in order to have more to eat. And in Yugoslavia the terms of trade turned in favor of agriculture by 20 per cent in the period 1956–61.[13] The significance of all this may be illustrated by supposing that a typical agricultural household produces 100 units of food grain and assuming that as a result of changes in relative prices its real income improves by 20 per cent. With an income elasticity of 0.859 the household increases its consumption of food grain from, say, 50 to 58.5 units $(0.859 \times .20 = .17; 50 \times .17 = 8.5; 50 + 8.5 = 58.5)$ and thus reduces the amount it sells from 50 to 41.5 units $(50 - 8.5 = 41.5)$.[14] This action on the part of the agricultural household reduces by almost one-sixth the supply of food grain available to others.

These are characteristics of very poor communities. As Schultz

[10] *Ibid.*, p. 54.
[11] Stipetić, *op. cit.*, p. 819.
[12] Schultz, *op. cit.*, p. 32.
[13] Stipetić, *op. cit.*, Table 1, p. 805.
[14] Schultz, *op. cit.*, p. 327.

correctly indicates, such a situation has very serious implications for the rest of the economy. What happens to a country's industrialization program when urban dwellers find their food supplies curtailed by price rises? The implications are indeed ominous.

Since income elasticities tend to change slowly over time, the foregoing results, if correct, may also shed light on the often-voiced criticism of the postwar government to the effect that the prewar "large" export surplus of Yugoslavian agricultural products, especially that of the 1930's, no longer seems to exist. For much of that period the terms of trade were unfavorable to agriculture and with an income elasticity somewhere in the foregoing range a "surplus" could indeed be generated but, as it seems, only at the expense of farmers' stomachs. If this is correct, criticism of the postwar government on this score loses much of its force. After all a fuller stomach, even if it is only that of a farmer, should also be counted as economic development.

I am, however, very skeptical about an income elasticity of 0.859 for agricultural households in Yugoslavia. It appears to me to be too high to serve as an accurate indicator of conditions in the Yugoslav countryside. My own rough estimates backed up by travels in the countryside in 1958, 1961, and 1963 would place the figure as somewhere between 0.6 and 0.7 for the period. An estimate as high as 0.859 would perhaps approximate conditions in Kosmet-Metohija, some areas of Macedonia, and perhaps Montenegro, but not in Slovenia, Vojvodina, Serbia, Croatia, and Bosnia-Hercegovina, where the bulk of the country's rural and also urban population is located.

Some idea of the effects of changes in population and income on the demand for farm products for the entire country can be obtained for the years 1956–61. The population during this period increased about 6 per cent, and income per capita increased roughly about 36 per cent. With an income elasticity for farm products of about 0.63, according to Stipetić, the demand for farm products increased by about 30 per cent.[15] Approximately 24 per

[15] *Ibid.*, p. 26.

cent of the increase in demand arose from the increase in per capita income, assuming other things unchanged and an average income elasticity of 0.63 over the entire increase in income. Six per cent of the increase in demand came from the increase in population.

Although these results are only approximate and admittedly rough, they do suggest a very large shift to the right in the demand schedule in a comparatively short period. This shift is about on a par with the increase in agricultural output that occurred at the same time. However, agricultural output during this period has tended to be spotty. In the drought years of 1958 and 1961 output declined. The average annual increase in agricultural output for the period according to Table 33 was approximately 5.2 per cent.

TABLE 33. Agricultural output indexes, 1957–61 (1955–56 = 100)

			Years			Average annual increase
Sectors	1957	1958	1959	1960	1961	
Total agricultural output	132	117	154	138	128	5.2%
Socialist sector	158	170	271	273	254	20.5%
Private sector	127	115	147	131	121	4.0%

Source: Stipetić, in *Ekonomski pregled*, no. 10–11 (1962), p. 808.

Much of this could be accounted for by the increase that occurred in the socialist sector, especially on large farms. The private sector accounted for a very modest increase indeed.

Such estimates, however, tend to underrate the importance of the private sector's role in the country's agriculture. Using Stipetić's estimates, I have computed an average annual value of the country's marketable agricultural output at 423 billion dinars for the years 1956–61. On the average about 355 billion dinars or 84 per cent of the marketable surplus was accounted for by the private sector of agriculture, though the socialist sector has been gaining in its share of this output since 1956. Some insight into the problems of agriculture in the private sector is provided by the fact that during this period an average of only 41 per cent of the total value of output was marketed. Moreover, this figure remained remarkably constant over the entire period. During the same period about 53 per cent of the total marketable agricultural output was placed on the market indirectly through various socialist organizations, and 47 per cent was sold directly on the market by private farmers.

Fortunately for Yugoslavia and its industrialization program outside food supplies have been available, primarily from American agricultural surpluses. Without such outside aid the country would have been hard pressed to continue its industrialization policies. Even in its most prosperous postwar period agricultural output did not quite manage to keep up with the growth in demand, much less generate an export surplus, which some development theorists argue is the *sine qua non* for economic development.

The rather spotty performance of the agricultural sector can be attributed to the fact that this sector has only been given consideration since the mid-1950's. Prior to that time, and to some degree even since, agriculture has apparently been regarded as a convenient well from which to pump resources into industrialization. Indeed in the years 1952 to 1956 the total investment in agriculture amounted to 21.7 billion dinars, which was less than was expended on agricultural equipment and machinery in 1957. According to Bogosavljević's estimates, which are summarized in Table 34, most of the investment resources since 1957 have been allocated to farm equipment and machinery. Livestock and land improvement also appear to have received favorable treatment.

The access of the agricultural sector to investment funds was facilitated in 1959 when the Yugoslav Agricultural Bank was established. Thenceforth the Agricultural Bank instead of the Investment Bank and National Bank allocated investment resources to agriculture. In 1960 the Bank established more adequate economic criteria for the allocation of investment funds. At the same time the repayment periods for most loans were reduced.

TABLE 34. Type of investment in agriculture, 1957–60 (*in billions of dinars*)

Type of investment	Year			
	1957	1958	1959	1960
Equipment and machinery	26.0	35.0	46.0	43.0
Seedlings	3.2	4.0	5.3	5.5
Livestock	8.5	10.0	12.8	15.0
Processing and storage	2.8	3.4	8.3	5.0
Land improvement	7.5	13.0	19.6	18.5
Farm buildings	1.2	2.5	13.8	13.3
Other	5.2	5.3	6.3	5.5

Source: M. Bogosavljević, *Economy of Yugoslavia* (Belgrade: Yugoslavia Publishing House, 1961), p. 28.

The objective was to force a more economic use of investment resources in agriculture.

Private and socialist segments of agriculture have apparently not had the same access to investment resources. Some steps to improve the situation occurred in 1957–58 when the investment fund available to general agricultural cooperatives was enlarged. These cooperatives as well as banks stood ready to advance short- and long-term loans to private farmers. For one reason or another farmers were hesitant to get involved to any great extent with the government. Some headway has been made in allaying farmers' suspicions of the government's efforts. To judge from the figures presented by Hoffman and Neal progress has been anything but spectacular.[16] In 1958, for instance, 738 million dinars of short-term credit and 2,100 million dinars of long-term credit were granted private farmers by banking organizations. This is in marked contrast to the 63 billion dinars of short-term credit and 42 billion dinars in long-term credit outstanding in the same year in the socialist sector of agriculture. Such a disparity is particularly interesting in indicating the seriousness of the problem when account is taken of the fact that the private sector encompasses about 90 per cent of the country's arable land.

[16] *Op. cit.,* p. 288.

The important role that favorable investment treatment has played in increasing the country's agricultural output is indicated by the performance of the several areas comprising this sector. Crop farming has advanced much faster than livestock breeding even though the farmer is more susceptible to climatic factors than the breeder. Grain farming, however, absorbed 58 per cent of the total public investment made in agriculture during the three years 1957, 1958, and 1959 compared to 22 per cent for livestock breeding. Comparatively small amounts were invested in horticulture and viniculture; indeed in the case of the latter the area planted to hybrid varieties of grapes was reduced during these years. In view of the comparatively high income elasticities of demand indicated in Table 32 for such items as meat and milk products it would seem that considerably more attention should be given to livestock breeding.

The fact that the socialist and private agricultural sectors have varied in the percentages of their increases in output again demonstrates the importance of investment in the country's agriculture. The socialist sector outstripped the performance of the private sector primarily because the socialist sector was favored in the investment program. The uncertainty surrounding the status of the private farmer decreased only after the 1953 reform. Thereafter private farmers began to gain some confidence in the security of their property and began to put into their holdings some of the meager resources at their disposal. Indeed, total private investment in agriculture jumped from 27 billion dinars in 1956 to 37 billion in 1957.

The performance of the private and socialist sectors is indicated by the yields of three staple crops: corn, wheat, and sugar beets. Table 35 shows the performance of these two sectors in the output of these three staple crops. The favorable investment treatment received by the socialist sector is indicated by the larger and more stable yields in comparison with those of the private sector. The steps that have been taken to improve the condition of private farmers in the form of general agricultural cooperatives have greatly improved the output of private farms. In Serbia, for

TABLE 35. Corn, wheat, and sugar beet yields in the socialist and private sectors, 1954–61 (*in metric centners per hectare*)

Year	Corn		Wheat		Sugar beets	
	SOCIALIST	PRIVATE	SOCIALIST	PRIVATE	SOCIALIST	PRIVATE
1954	18.4	11.6	9.3	7.3	175.2	153.5
1955	19.9	15.5	17.5	12.0	193	199
1956	21.4	12.7	15.0	9.5	171	160
1957	38.4	20.8	23.0	15.2	286	234
1958	40.3	14.8	22.8	11.4	258	188
1959	49.9	24.0	38.9	17.3	331	276
1960	45.4	54.1	30.6	36.3	337	515
1961	34.8	40.8	30.5	34.1	248	383

Source: National Bank of Yugoslavia, *Statistical Bulletins*, nos. 42, 68, 71, 129, 151, 217, 240, and 273 for the years 1954, 1955, 1956, 1957, 1958, 1959, 1960, and 1961, respectively.

example, average wheat yields on nonmember private farms were 25 metric centners per hectare in 1959 and 39 metric centners per hectare on private farms that were members of the cooperatives.

The socialist sector and the part of the private sector cooperating with it comprised about 19 per cent of the total area sown in 1959. The apparent success of the cooperative movement is indicated by the fact that the number of private holdings cooperating with the socialist sector rose from 24,770 in 1957 to 207,849 in 1958, while the total acreage tilled under such cooperation increased from 20,561 to 174,931 hectares. There were 2,230 private holdings with a total of 1,675 hectares that cooperated with the socialist sector in viniculture and horticulture in 1957. The number of individual holdings that entered into forms of association with cooperative organizations in the sector of livestock farming rose from 27,103 in 1957 to 70,210 in 1958.

13.

FOREIGN TRADE

THEORY OF COMPARATIVE ADVANTAGE
AND ECONOMIC DEVELOPMENT

According to received doctrine, the theory of comparative advantage is an argument for a country to specialize in the production of those commodities that require the use of its relatively abundant factors. The static nature of the theory, however, does not invalidate its use in countries undergoing economic development. Changing conditions merely provide new bases for comparative advantage. For example, if capital accumulation proceeds faster in one country than in others, the factor endowments underlying comparative advantage as well as the comparative advantage itself change. The basis for trade is changed. A new basis, however, does exist.

The opponents of comparative advantage must overcome the preference given by theory to specialization. Received theory argues that, all other things being equal, an incremental balanced unit of resources ought to be allocated to the export industries in the broad sense rather than to import-competing industries because the country is more efficient in the production of the export commodities. As a result more of the import goods can be obtained by producing the export goods and trading.

Attempts to dispute the theory and its conclusions have taken many forms. The more important appear to be the infant industry arguments, short-term instability in the export trade, long-term behavior of the terms of trade, disparity between social and private costs, irrelevance of the classic two-country, two-commodity world to the real world of factor movements, capital accumulation, the issue of intermediate goods, and changing technology. In spite of these arguments, however, the fact of the matter is that foreign trade is capable of giving considerable assistance to developing countries. And indeed on occasion it has provided the stimulus to the economic development of a country, such as Great Britain.

There are at least three foreign trade models that should receive serious consideration by a developing country.[1] In one model the export industry represents a leading sector; in another it represents the lagging sector; and in the third it serves as a balancing sector. The first model makes the country less dependent on internal balance but more sensitive to external events. The second model emphasizes internal development as a means for cushioning, if not avoiding, external shocks that would subsequently slow down internal development. The third model reduces the pressure on a country to maintain balance in its internal development as, for example, between agriculture and industry.

Since economic development is possible by way of any of the models, even in relatively closed economies, the problem turns on selecting the model or the combination most appropriate to a given country. The proper solution will be determined by the types and qualities of resources available. If the resources in a country are highly specialized, more can probably be gained from foreign trade than will be lost through the risks and possible instability generated by such trade. This is usually the case in countries with small geographic areas. On the other hand, if the country possesses a wide variety of resources both natural and human, as in the case of large continental countries, foreign trade loses some of its significance for the country. In either case, however, a country can benefit from international trade and participation in the international division of labor.

This does not mean that a small country embarked on an

[1] See, for example, the discussion in Charles P. Kindleberger, *Economic Development* (New York: McGraw-Hill, 1958), pp. 245 ff.

economic development program has little choice but to accept the lagging trade model because of the assertion that it can do little to increase the external demand for its products. This is incorrect for at least two reasons. In the first place, it can push exports of manufactures, for example, to replace the declining agricultural sector if this was the source of its previous exports. In the second place, if exports can be made cheaper through increased investment and technological advance, it may be possible to stimulate exports to the extent that they in fact lead the development process itself. It is difficult for a developing country to plan its exports, which in fact involves planning another country's imports. Too often the problem is solved by examining lists of imports to see which of the commodities can be replaced by domestic production. Such a solution, unfortunately, fails to examine the export list for the purpose of ascertaining the commodities whose costs could be lowered and for which an external demand already exists.

FOREIGN LOANS AND GRANTS: A SOURCE OF ADDITIONAL RESOURCES

There is a notion that is popular but of limited validity that borrowing abroad makes development possible by providing the country with certain selected resources, as for example capital goods not available domestically. This view is correct only insofar as a country's economy is severely restricted in its ability to transform and so redirect resources from one sector to another. Restrictions on transformation are more likely to occur in the short run when, for example, the economy is unable to shift resources to the production of needed capital goods. In effect, this notion is the result of inappropriately applying partial equilibrium analysis to a general equilibrium problem.

The general solution is that borrowing abroad should be thought of as a means for adding to the total resources of all kinds, including consumption goods, at the disposal of the economy. Foreign borrowing can take the form of purchasing consumption goods abroad, thereby releasing domestic resources for the construction of capital goods, e.g., domestic building.

Much discussion has been expended in development literature on the twin issues of capacity to absorb capital and capacity to repay. At times these discussions confuse partial with general equilibrium solutions. The International Bank for Reconstruction and Development, among others, has in effect asserted that the problem of development is not so much the supply of capital as it is the inability of developing countries to absorb capital. The Bank's criterion for determining capacity to absorb is apparently the existence of well-planned and productive bankable projects that are an integral part of the country's development program. The difficulty with this view is that it must of necessity be a short-run view in which economic transformation is limited. Furthermore, if the Bank's criterion is taken seriously, a country with rigid central planning would be more likely to qualify for a loan than one that shuns such planning and emphasizes the allocation of resources through the free market.

A general equilibrium view of the capacity to absorb capital suggests that it is unlimited. Arbitrary limits can, of course, be set, but if "productive projects" are interpreted as those that yield a positive return above the cost of capital and if time is allowed for transformation to occur, the capacity to absorb capital can indeed be unlimited. More particularly, if consumption is also allowed out of capital, the Bank's problems would be quickly solved.

There are, of course, situations in which the capacity argument does make some sense. An example is provided in cases of complementary factors. The inability of such factors to keep pace with each other does limit the ability of the economy to absorb capital. The development of modern factories, for example, needs skilled manpower, new universities require professors, and so on.

It is important to distinguish short-run and long-run factors affecting a country's capacity to repay. In the long run the only seriously limiting factors to the capacity to repay are the debt's contribution to the economy's productivity, the ability of the country's fiscal system to raise the necessary resources for repayment, and the ease of transformation whereby resources are diverted into export-increasing activities. In the short run the capacity to repay is governed largely by the foreign exchange requirements of investments undertaken.

Failure to distinguish between the short-run and the long-run implications of foreign borrowing and repayment has led recipient governments to favor external resources in the form of grants rather than loans for the construction of overhead capital. Grants are essentially short-run affairs. Direct government grants are usually favored, principally because such grants tend to pay little attention to the over-all productivity of the economy and the time factor necessary to achieve the required transformation in the economy.

Other sources of confusion in foreign borrowing arise from the alleged fears of underdeveloped countries that as a consequence of such borrowing they will be at the "mercy of foreign investors." This is particularly true in the case of private foreign investment. It has led many of these countries to impose unnecessary rules and regulations concerning such investment. One particularly erroneous notion is held by some countries that favor only those foreign investors who invest in manufacturing. The source of the confusion here, of course, is identifying manufacturing with economic development. To this may be added the fears of so-called socialist countries that private investment would undermine the existing internal *status quo*. Private investors are not likely to look with fondness on grandiose governmental projects that tend to lose money.

To fill the postwar gap in private foreign investment, created for the most part by the underdeveloped countries themselves, recourse has been had to various international organizations such as the International Bank for Reconstruction and Development. The Bank through its arrangements with recipient countries has facilitated the flow of some private investment. Other arrangements to fill the gap are more or less unilateral in nature. The most notable, of course, are government-to-government loans and grants.

Perhaps the most novel way of obtaining foreign resources for development is through foreign agricultural surpluses, principally

American. This method of borrowing is more sophisticated than others in that it rejects the notion that borrowing should take the form of capital goods. The resources thus displaced in domestic agriculture can be shifted to other sectors, including the production of capital goods. And indeed even if such resources are not displaced, the acquisition of agricultural surpluses may release foreign exchange for the purchase of other consumer goods or capital equipment. Perhaps most important to recipient countries with lagging agricultural sectors is the fact that receipt of agricultural surpluses enables a country to achieve some semblance of balance in its internal development. The relief provided by these surpluses may very well prevent serious balance-of-payment problems arising out of the inability of domestic agriculture to generate food surpluses. At the same time it encourages domestic capital formation, thereby allowing development to proceed.

THE CHANGING CHARACTER OF COMPARATIVE ADVANTAGE IN YUGOSLAVIA

Insofar as the composition of exports and imports is a useful indicator of a country's comparative advantage, the postwar evidence suggests that the basis for Yugoslavia's foreign trade has changed. The volume of industrial products exported has been increasing while that of agricultural products has been declining. The change, however, has not been steady. The evidence summarized in Table 36 suggests that only after 1952 did the volume

TABLE 36. Average volume of exports of industrial, agricultural, and timber products for selected years (*in billions of dinars and 1955 prices*)

Years	Industry	Agriculture	Forestry
1935–39	46.3	37.3	4.5
1947–51	41.2	11.6	4.7
1952–56	51.3	20.0	4.2

Source: Computed from *Foreign Trade Statistics of FRP Yugoslavia* (Belgrade: Yugoslav Bank for Foreign Trade, for relevant years).

of industrial exports manage to surge ahead of that of the prewar period. The low status of agriculture, which, as we have seen, was not so low before the war, is indicated by the fact that it has not managed to recover even its prewar volume in the country's foreign trade. These figures once again underscore the shifting of resources away from agriculture to industry that has occurred in the postwar period. Such shifts have had the inevitable consequence of changing the country's comparative advantage and so the basis for foreign trade. The answer to the question of whether or not the postwar shifts represent a real comparative advantage or a forced one is not clear-cut. Other things being equal, postwar events in the country certainly argue that it is in part a forced one. But other things are not equal, particularly in the postwar world market. How well, for example, could Yugoslav agricultural exports have competed on the world market in the face of American agricultural surpluses?

The changing bases for trade are indicated not only by industrial export volume but also by the pattern of exports. Not only has the volume of industrial exports increased, but entire new branches of activity have begun to play an important role in postwar trade. The export of various types of equipment is illustrative. Up to 1956, for example, the products of shipbuilding hardly ever made the export list, and the products of the metal-processing and electrical manufacturing industry were negligible in the export trade, constituting only 0.3 per cent of the total exports in 1939 and 1952. In 1956 their percentage increased to 6 per cent, and in 1959 this percentage jumped to 23 per cent. This is indeed a significant change for a country which before the war exported chiefly nonferrous metals, timber, and livestock.

Additional insight into the changing pattern of exports is provided by the evidence summarized in Table 37 on the degree of finish of exports. These figures suggest a rapid rise in the export of finished manufactures and a decline in the export of crude articles and semimanufactures. The more detailed breakdown of exports according to international classification presented in Table 38 is also instructive in suggesting the country's changing bases for

TABLE 37. Exports according to degree of finish

Articles	Percentage of participation			
	1952	1956	1959	1962
Crude articles	50.5	36.7	25.4	19.6
Semimanufactures	42.8	42.8	37.0	37.6
Finished manufactures	6.7	20.5	37.6	42.8
Total	100.0	100.0	100.0	100.0

Source: *Yugoslav Survey*, Sept. 1960, p. 231, and *Statistics of Foreign Trade of the SFR, Yugoslavia, 1962*.

trade. The evidence supports the conclusion that finished products are growing in importance in the export trade.

The changing composition of the import trade reinforces the conclusions reached regarding the changing basis for trade. Although exports have been increasing, imports have surged ahead at an even faster pace. The increasing tempo of domestic activity has manifested itself in raising imports. Thus imports during the 1947–51 period, when domestic activity was at a low ebb, were only 2 per cent greater than during the period 1935–39. By 1952–56, however, when domestic activity picked up, imports

TABLE 38. Exports according to international classification (*in billions of dinars at current prices*)

Exports	1952	1956	1959	1962
Total exports	74.0	97.0	143.0	207.3
Food	28.2	24.9	36.5	48.3
Beverages and tobacco	2.9	7.9	7.1	9.0
Raw materials, inedible	19.4	22.9	22.8	28.7
Mineral fuels and lubricants	1.2	1.3	1.5	5.3
Chemicals	2.9	4.3	4.7	6.5
Manufactured goods classified by materials	18.1	26.8	35.5	46.8
Machinery and transport equipment	—	4.5	24.8	47.3
Miscellaneous mfg. articles	0.5	3.5	8.7	15.2
Miscellaneous transactions	0.8	0.9	1.4	0.2

Source: *Yugoslav Survey*, Sept. 1960, p. 231, and *Index* (Belgrade), 1963, no. 2.

increased by 46 per cent compared to the previous five-year period. They surged to an unprecedented 68 per cent rise over the average of 1952–56 during 1957–58. Up to 1956 the annual rise in imports proceeded at an annual rate of about 6.9. During 1957–59, however, the annual rate rose about 14.3 per cent.

Table 39 illustrating the composition of imports suggests the important role that consumer goods, equipment, semifinished goods, and raw materials play in the country's imports. And such a role has been growing in importance. During the years 1947–51 the volume of imports of raw materials and semifinished goods

TABLE 39. Imports according to allotment (*averages in billions of dinars at 1955 prices*)

Period	Raw materials and semifinished goods	Investment goods	Consumer goods
1935–39	48.5	14.3	17.5
1947–51	51.9	20.2	9.4
1952–56	61.0	28.0	32.2

Source: *Yugoslav Survey*, Sept. 1961, p. 233.

averaged only about 7 per cent above the prewar level even though by 1951 industrial output had increased by over 66 per cent compared to 1939. By 1952–56 this import category increased on an average about 17 per cent. Even so, this rise was insufficient, and domestic development of such branches as processing was retarded. More favorable conditions developed in 1957–59, when the category of raw materials and semifinished goods expanded by about 77 per cent over the years 1952–56. Much of the expansion in the category of imports during 1957–59 is accounted for by textile fibers and related items, leather and rubber, technical fats, artificial fertilizers, rolled goods, assembly parts for metal processing, electrical goods, and components for the shipbuilding industry.

The category "investment goods" or equipment has been particularly important in postwar imports. Indeed the import of equipment during the entire postwar period has accounted for about one-fifth of the country's total imports. By 1957–59 equipment imports rose by 68 per cent in comparison with those of the previous five-year period. Many changes, however, have occurred in the pattern of equipment imports during recent years. The importation of complete installations has declined while at the same time individual components of machinery have increased. This is consistent with the tendency already noted to export finished products. Imports of farm machinery and transportation equipment in particular have increased in recent years reflecting in part the growing attempts to rectify the sad state of affairs in these two branches of the economy.

Consumer goods constitute another growing category of imports. From the low postwar point reached in 1947–50 when they constituted only about 6 to 9 per cent of total imports, they rose until in 1957–59 they comprised almost a third of total imports. Indeed during 1957–59 imports of foodstuffs alone constituted about 23 per cent of the total value of imports owing in part to domestic crop failures as a result of the 1958 drought.

Our examination of the country's imports and exports suggests that Yugoslavia has not quite fallen into the error, as have some developing countries, of insisting that imports of capital equipment take precedence over all other categories, including consumption goods. It has, however, come dangerously close. The country does not seem to be driven by a desire for autarchy or self-sufficiency. Indeed, the opposite appears to be the case. There is apparently a desire, if not yet altogether realized, to participate in the international division of labor. Such a desire has serious implications for the course of economic planning. This will be discussed in the next chapter.

The geographic pattern of Yugoslav foreign trade is in itself revealing as to the country's wish to mesh its economy with that of other countries. It conducts trade with virtually every country in the world. The evidence given in Table 40 on the distribution of exports and imports indicates, however, that most of its foreign

TABLE 40. Distribution of exports and imports according to geographic area in selected years (*in millions of dinars at current prices*)

	1948				1952				1956				1959				1962			
	Exports		Imports		Exports		Imports		Exports		Imports		Exports		Imports		Exports		Imports	
	AMT.	% OF TOTAL	AMT.	% OF TOTAL	AMT.	% OF TOTAL	AMT.	% OF TOTAL	AMT.	% OF TOTAL	AMT.	% OF TOTAL	AMT.	% OF TOTAL	AMT.	% OF TOTAL	AMT.	% OF TOTAL	AMT.	% OF TOTAL
Total	89.1	100	91.9	100	74.0	100	111.9	100	97.0	100	142.2	100	143.0	100	206.2	100	207.1	100.0	266.3	100.0
West Europe	36.4	41	40.7	44	58.2	78	76.6	68	54.4	56	55.5	39	65.3	46	86.8	42	91.2	44.0	120.6	45.3
East Europe	44.6	50	41.9	45	—	—	—	—	22.2	23	31.5	22	44.1	31	50.9	25	49.8	24.1	57.0	21.4
Asia	1.9	2	—	—	1.3	2	1.7	2	5.9	6	2.2	1	14.0	10	12.1	6	24.1	11.6	20.0	7.5
Africa	3.4	4	3.5	4	2.2	3	4.0	4	2.6	2	7.6	5	7.4	5	6.2	3	14.1	6.8	7.0	2.6
North America	2.4	3	3.2	4	10.9	15	26.5	23	8.5	9	40.5	29	10.3	7	42.7	21	18.6	9.0	56.4	21.2
South America	0.4	0.5	2.4	3	1.3	2	1.1	1	3.4	4	3.9	3	1.9	1	4.6	2	9.3	4.5	3.7	1.4
Other countries	—	—	0.2	—	0.1	0	2.0	2	—	—	1.0	1	—	—	2.9	1	0.0	0.0	1.6	0.6

Source: *Foreign Trade Statistics of FPR Yugoslavia* for relevant years; for 1962 figures, Research Department, National Bank of Yugoslavia.

trade is carried on with European countries. The foremost place, amounting to over 40 per cent, is held by Western Europe. In view of the development of the Common Market such a pattern holds significant economic and possibly political implications for the country; these will be discussed later. Trade with Eastern Europe, though it has recovered somewhat, has not reached the pre-1948 level. Moreover, it is not equally heavy with all of the countries in Eastern Europe.

Significant expansion in trade has occurred with Asia and Africa. Exports to countries in these two areas have increased from about 6 per cent of total exports in 1948 to about 15 per cent in 1959, while the volume of exports to these areas has increased fourfold in the same period. Imports from Afro-Asian areas increased almost fivefold in 1959 as compared to 1948. Much of this rise consists of direct purchases of raw materials. There is every indication that trade with Afro-Asian areas will increase. These trends in trade reflect in part the Yugoslav foreign policy of political nonalignment.

Trade with North America is principally trade with the United States. The rather substantial import volume consists mainly of purchases with assistance funds and farm surpluses. This trade gained in momentum after 1951 with the import of staple foodstuffs. Indeed, over the years such commodities have comprised more than one-third of the total imports of Yugoslavia. Exports to the North American area have not increased as spectacularly as have imports, though there is hope that exports can be increased.

The number of Yugoslavia's trading partners has been increasing. Whereas in 1948 Yugoslavia exported to 61 countries and imported from 50, by 1959 it exported to 83 countries and imported from 78. Table 41 shows the country's top ten trading partners. The changing ranks of the countries in the table suggest that the area with which Yugoslavia has been trading has expanded since 1948. Such an expansion has the effect of increasing the country's participation in the international division of labor while at the same time safeguarding its economy against possible disturbances in the markets of any given geographic area.

TABLE 41. The top ten countries and their percentages of Yugoslavia's foreign trade

Countries	1948		1956		1959		1962	
	Exports	Imports	Exports	Imports	Exports	Imports	Exports	Imports
Austria	6.1 (8) *	4.7 (7)	5.3 (6)	4.1 (6)	4.4 (8)	3.8 (8)	3.9 (8)	3.6 (7)
Belgium	—	5.4 (6)	—	—	—	—	—	—
Czechoslovakia	15.9 (1)	17.1 (1)	—	2.5 (8)	3.4 (9)	3.3 (9)	3.1 (9)	2.9 (9)
East Germany	—	4.2 (10)	—	—	5.6 (7)	4.2 (7)	5.1 (7)	4.1 (5)
Egypt	3.3 (10)	—	—	—	—	—	3.1 (10)	—
France	—	—	2.7 (10)	2.9 (7)	—	—	—	—
Great Britain	6.2 (7)	4.6 (8)	6.0 (5)	6.9 (5)	7.1 (4)	5.1 (5)	7.1 (4)	3.0 (8)
Greece	—	—	3.0 (8)	—	3.0 (10)	—	—	—
Holland	6.4 (6)	7.3 (5)	—	—	—	—	—	—
Hungary	9.0 (3)	4.4 (9)	—	—	—	4.6 (6)	—	2.4 (10)
Italy	8.1 (4)	10.7 (3)	14.2 (2)	8.7 (4)	12.1 (1)	9.3 (3)	14.0 (1)	11.8 (2)
Poland	7.8 (5)	7.4 (4)	2.8 (9)	1.6 (10)	7.0 (5)	3.0 (10)	6.1 (6)	3.6 (6)
Soviet Union	15.0 (2)	10.8 (2)	13.1 (3)	14.9 (2)	9.9 (2)	8.4 (4)	6.3 (5)	6.7 (4)
Switzerland	3.4 (9)	—	5.0 (7)	2.2 (9)	—	—	—	—
United States	—	—	8.5 (4)	27.3 (1)	6.5 (6)	20.4 (1)	7.5 (3)	20.6 (1)
West Germany	—	—	15.3 (1)	10.0 (3)	9.4 (3)	14.0 (2)	10.3 (2)	11.2 (3)
Total %	81.2	76.6	75.9	81.1	68.4	76.1	66.5	69.9

Source: *Yugoslav Survey*, Sept. 1960, p. 236, and Research Department, National Bank of Yugoslavia.
* Figures in ( ) indicate rankings of country.

14.

EXCHANGE RATE AND THE
BALANCE OF PAYMENTS

EXCHANGE RATE REFORMS

In 1961 positive steps were taken to abolish the cumbersome and complicated exchange rate system. The previous system calling for a rate of exchange of 300 dinars to a dollar overvalued the dinar and led to the use of so-called coefficients which in effect were a system of multiple exchange rates. By 1954 a new disparity rate of 632 dinars was being applied to all commodity transactions, and twelve import and thirteen export coefficients were in existence. In addition, there were three other exchange rates: a tourist rate of 400 dinars to the dollar, another for invisible items of 600 dinars to the dollar, and a third which, in effect, was a sort of free market rate. In 1961 all of this was brushed aside and a single rate of 750 dinars to the dollar was established. Customs duties replaced the cumbersome system of coefficients. The new tariff is based on duties ad valorem, with the rate going as high as 60 per cent of the value of imported goods.

The importance of the foreign exchange and trade reforms is suggested by the fact that almost one-fifth of the country's income depends on international trade and that fraction is expected to increase. Ostensibly the reforms are motivated by a desire to increase the role of the market and at the same time decrease direct governmental intervention in economic activity.[1]

Yugoslavia is, however, a long way from adopting Great Britain's nineteenth-century free-trade doctrine. On the contrary, serious consideration continues to be given to the so-called infant industry argument for protection. The application of protection apparently is to be severely restricted in the future. Under the 1961 reforms only temporary protection in the form of customs tariffs and subsidies will be given industries seeking protection, and such recipients must first demonstrate that they can quickly meet foreign competition. Furthermore, no protection or subsidies will be given to industries with obsolete equipment and low productivity. They will be permitted to fall by the wayside. There is little doubt but that these reforms, if they are permitted their full play, will enable foreign trade to exercise a positive influence in strengthening the competitive position of the Yugoslav economy.

As a result of the 1961 reforms, methods for allocating foreign exchange have improved. They too are based, or so it seems, on increasing the role of the price system at the expense of direct governmental intervention. Though the regulations on exchange allocation have been reduced, they have not been eliminated. Thus the purchase of foreign exchange for imports by economic organizations depends on the classification of commodities to be imported. Appendix 2 presents the various classifications. For commodities on the freely importable list, for example, foreign exchange can be purchased from authorized banks in unlimited quantities. For other commodities there are varying degrees of restriction according to the methods of import. For example, in the case of commodities imported on the basis of a general permit to import, the amount of foreign exchange that can be bought is determined by a percentage of the amount of foreign exchange that the economic organization under consideration used for import purposes in the preceding year. In 1961 an organization

---

[1] "Decree on Foreign Exchange Operations," *Official Gazette of FPRY*, no. 2, 1961.

could use 80 per cent of the amount of foreign exchange it spent in 1960. From this sum, however, deductions are made of the amount of foreign exchange it spent on imports of goods contained in the lists of free imports, on imports against "liberalized permits," and on imports of "quota articles." In case the organization does not use the full amount of its foreign exchange the balance can be carried forward and used in the next year. Organizations desiring to import above the established percentage can make special arrangements to buy foreign exchange from authorized banks. In such cases the bank evaluates the profitability of the undertaking in which the foreign exchange is to be employed.

For imports of quota commodities special foreign exchange funds are available. Authorized banks publish the amounts and types of foreign exchange available and the deadlines for submitting applications. Individual enterprises can conclude agreements among themselves regarding the allocation of foreign exchange in such funds. The bank automatically allocates the exchange on the basis of the agreement. If the enterprises cannot reach an agreement, the allocation of the quota is made by an authorized governmental body, which is influenced by such considerations as the desire to decrease imports and increase exports, balance-of-payments effects, and the general economic effects of the projects.

Extraordinary foreign exchange quotas are available to export organizations in proportion to their own contribution to the country's foreign exchange earnings. Foreign exchange earned can be applied in specified ways to cover an enterprise's expenses as well as to purchase commodities used in its economic activity. For example, exporters of agricultural products receive 3 per cent of realized foreign exchange earnings; exporters of industrial products, international transport services, board and lodging services, and travel agencies receive 7 per cent; exporters of game, medicinal herbs, books, magazines, musical scores, and domestic films receive 25 per cent.

Foreign exchange for imports of consumer goods is made available according to the classification of the commodities to be imported. Some idea of the claim that consumer goods have on foreign exchange can be obtained from Appendix 2. Needless to say, the claim is not as great as it is for the import of capital equipment. Exchange for the import of capital equipment is obtained from authorized banks on the basis of contracts and in accordance with other established regulations. For such imports enterprises can also use the foreign exchange obtained for imports against general permits as well as a percentage of their foreign exchange earnings. An import permit is required if the desired capital equipment is on the list of restricted imports. Foreign exchange for the import of equipment can also be obtained equal in amount to a specified percentage of the dinar depreciation allowance of the enterprise. For example, in economic enterprises belonging to the Association of Yugoslav Railways such an allowance equals 5 per cent of total depreciation funds; for mines, foundries, and machine-building, port, and storage firms in sea transportation the figure is 2 per cent; for crude oil production firms it is 8 per cent; for warehousing it is 10 per cent; for river transportation it is 14 per cent; for air transportation it is 30 per cent; for all other organizations in trade and industry it is 1 per cent; for economic organizations in agriculture it is 20 per cent of the depreciation fund for the current year.

Table 42 shows the country's balance of payments in 1959 and 1960. An examination of these suggests a characteristic familiar throughout the 1950's, namely, that the country's balance-of-payment deficit originated primarily as a deficit in its balance of trade.

The continuing rise in the balance-of-trade deficit was partially offset by improvement in the balance of invisible transactions. This is the continuation of a trend established in 1954. Receipts in invisible transactions in 1960 grew substantially and represent mainly growth in maritime and railway transport receipts occasioned, in part, by the expansion of the Yugoslav merchant marine. Larger receipts in the same year from insurance and other items suggest the developing economic ties with other countries. More moderate gains have been registered in tourism and emigrant remittances. Though their gains are modest, the various

TABLE 42. Balance of payments, 1959–62 (*in billions of dinars*)

	Resources				Payments				Balance			
	1959	1960	1961	1962	1959	1960	1961	1962	1959	1960	1961	1962
Current Account												
Exports, imports	145.7	172.6	174.4	209.7	211.3	253.8	278.7	270.0	−65.6	−81.2	−81.2	−60.2
Transport, insurance, and other	27.0	33.1	40.0	45.9	10.8	12.8	17.0	20.0	+16.2	+20.3	+20.3	+25.9
interest	0.3	0.4	0.2	1.2	3.4	3.7	5.6	7.5	−3.1	−3.3	−3.3	−6.4
Other invisibles	11.4	12.3	14.1	22.2	6.0	5.9	8.2	7.5	+5.4	+6.4	+6.4	+14.7
Gold (nonmonetary)	0.5	0.5	0.5	0.5	—	—	—	—	+0.5	0.5	+0.5	+0.5
Total	184.9	218.9	229.2	279.5	231.5	276.2	309.5	305.0	−46.6	−57.3	−57.3	−25
Financial Account												
Deficit in balance of payments	—	—	—	—	46.4	57.3	80.3	25.5	−46.6	−57.3	−57.3	−25.5
Foreign exchange reserves	6.9	6.6	—	—	—	—	16.0	6.5	+6.9	+6.6	+6.6	−6.5
Reparation and restitution payments	9.9	7.1	3.3	4.2	—	—	—	—	+9.9	+7.1	+7.1	+4.2
Government and private donation	14.1	9.8	7.3	7.1	1.2	0.9	0.9	0.9	+12.9	+8.9	+8.9	+6.2
Loans and credits	37.7	41.4	83.4	56.7	8.7	8.7	5.1	7.9	+29.0	+32.7	+32.7	+48.8
Transitory credits and debts	3.6	—	24.0	1.5	12.9	3.7	8.5	32.5	−9.3	−3.7	−3.7	−31.0
Clearing debts	1.7	2.2	—	2.3	—	—	6.2	—	+1.7	+2.2	+2.2	+2.3
Errors and omissions	—	3.5	—	1.5	4.5	—	1.0	—	−4.5	+3.5	+3.5	+1.5
Total	73.9	70.6	118.0	73.3	73.9	70.6	118.0	73.3	—	—	—	—

Source: National Bank of Yugoslavia, *Annual Report, 1960 and 1961* (Belgrade: The Bank, 1961 and 1962), pp. 60 (*1960*) and 67 (*1961*); 1962 figures are from the Research Department of the Bank.

invisible items could, if properly cultivated, provide the country with important sources of foreign exchange earnings.

Along with the increase in the balance-of-trade deficit, another potentially serious source of trouble was manifested in 1960 when there occurred a rise in the outflow of the already modest supply of foreign exchange. This is the consequence of the growing imbalance in the past few years between the inflow and outflow of convertible currencies. Such developments are indicators of the difficulty that the economy has been experiencing in carrying out necessary transformations. The large expenditures in convertible currency for capital equipment were not offset by the country's growing exports to the hard currency areas from which the equipment came. And, indeed, if United States agriculture surpluses are set aside because these transactions are carried out as special credits in dinars and thus have no impact on foreign exchange reserves, the deficit in convertible currencies in 1960 amounted to 34.9 billion dinars against 12.7 billion dinars in 1959.[2]

The critical nature of the situation is indicated by the fact that in 1960 foreign exchange reserves declined below the limit of an average one-month payment requirement, an amount that is far from sufficient to cover current foreign exchange operations. Moreover, much of the available foreign exchange represented credit balances on clearing accounts that have very limited application and so should not be included, strictly speaking, in foreign exchange reserves. In the view of some observers this depletion represents a serious obstacle to the operation of a more liberal foreign trade and exchange system. Yet such a system is indispensable to the country if it is to participate effectively in the international division of labor.

The recurring balance-of-payment deficits in earlier years were met from such sources as economic aid and reparations payments. These, however, began to dry up in 1960. Total receipts from these so-called extraordinary foreign resources amounted to 10.0 billion

[2] National Bank of Yugoslavia, *Annual Report 1960* (Belgrade: National Bank of Yugoslavia, 1960), p. 62.

dinars in 1960 against 14.6 billion dinars in 1959. Economic aid was 2.9 billion dinars, of which 2.5 billion dinars came from the United States in the form of agricultural surpluses.

Foreign borrowing is beginning to play an increasingly important role as a means of easing the country's foreign trade problems.[3] In 1959, for example, Yugoslavia concluded an agreement with the United States for a loan of $5.15 million, with Great Britain for one of 3 million pounds sterling, and with Italy for $50 million worth of credit. In 1960 two loans, one for $14.8 million and the other for $23 million were granted to Yugoslavia out of the United States Development Loan Fund. In 1961 the United States, Great Britain, France, Italy, and West Germany together with the International Monetary Fund granted Yugoslavia credit amounting to over $200 million for the purpose of easing its transition to a single exchange rate. Table 43 presents data on foreign loans, credits, and other liabilities for 1959 and 1960.

The repayment of investment loans, credits, and other consolidated claims which reached 17.0 billion dinars in 1960 compared to 14.7 billion dinars in 1959 is beginning to test the Yugoslav economy's capacity to repay. That the Yugoslav economy thus far leaves something to be desired on this score is indicated by the fact that the repayment issue is considered one of the country's basic balance-of-payment problems.[4]

Resort to longer-term loans and credits coupled with the negotiation of agreements on commodity deliveries between Yugoslavia and several countries provides additional time for the economy to undertake the necessary transformation to facilitate repayment. These agreements on commodity deliveries represent a type of credit advanced between Yugoslavia and a large number of countries in Asia and Africa as well as some South American and European countries. The Yugoslavs apparently hope that such credits will expand the country's external markets and so provide desperately needed foreign exchange. At best this is a long-term

[3] *Ibid.*, p. 63.
[4] *Ibid.*, p. 64.

TABLE 43. Foreign loans, credits, and other liabilities,* 1959, 1960, 1961, and 1962 (*in billions of dinars*)

Types of loans, credits, and other liabilities	Position on Dec. 31, 1959	Increase of debt in 1960	Repayment in 1960	Position on Dec. 31, 1960	Position on Dec. 31, 1961	Increase of debt in 1962	Repayment in 1962	Position on Dec. 31, 1962
(1) Foreign exchange loan	9.0	—	—	9.0	9.0	—	—	9.0
(2) Investment loans	38.8	3.7	3.0	39.5	42.2	5.3	3.4	44.1
(3) Investment credits	19.9	14.4	5.4	29.0 †	41.4	24.1	13.3	52.2
(4) Commodity credits	7.2	—	1.0	6.2	18.5	12.8	4.5	26.8
(5) Medium-term credits	26.0	0.8	4.6	22.2	41.8	4.7	2.3	44.2
(6) Liabilities in respect of nationalized property of foreign owners	6.4	1.1 ‡	0.8	6.7	5.9	—	0.7	5.2
(7) Other liabilities	5.9	1.0	2.2	3.2	2.9	—	1.3	3.2
Total	113.2	21.0	17.0	115.8	161.7	46.9	25.5	184.7

Source: National Bank of Yugoslavia, *Annual Report, 1960*, p. 64. The 1961 and 1962 figures are from the Research Department of the Bank.
* Data on special credits repayable in domestic currency and on short-term banking and commercial credits are not included.
† This item includes, in addition to the increase of liabilities in 1960, also the amount of outstanding commercial bills with prolonged repayment terms.
‡ The liabilities for nationalized property increased following the agreement with Turkey in 1960.

process. At its worst Yugoslavia is providing the signatory countries with hard currencies. This is done through the medium of its exports of machinery and related manufactures which are obtained by Yugoslavia through loans and grants from the hard currency areas. In return for these exports it receives inconvertible currency.

FLEXIBLE EXCHANGE RATES AND
ECONOMIC PLANNING

Many of the difficulties that Yugoslavia is experiencing in its foreign trade are of domestic origin. In the first place, the significant increases in the money stock and the elimination of the severe distortion in relative prices over the past few years have had their impact on internal prices and the balance of payments. In the second place, the country provides an illustration of the obstacles encountered by a small country conducting internal economic planning while heavily dependent on foreign trade. The problems involved in attempting to plan another country's imports and resulting from the availability of foreign loans and credits should be obvious to even the most ardent planner. Like it or not, a small country is subject to the economic sanctions of world markets.

An important source of difficulties for a country such as Yugoslavia is the official and rigid exchange rate that in 1961 replaced the system of multiple exchange rates. To judge from Yugoslavia's continuing balance-of-payment problem the reforms have only dealt with surface manifestations of more fundamental problems. Future changes in the exchange rate can be expected unless the country's foreign economic position improves significantly. But there is no mechanism for assuring that future changes will be of the required magnitude. Resort to other means to maintain equilibrium is likely only to intensify the country's problems. Loss of monetary reserves, changes in internal prices and incomes, direct controls, and similar measures are hardly profitable approaches for a country that apparently aspires to expand its external trade.

A flexible or floating exchange rate with its corollary of free convertibility may very well be a solution for at least a number of

Yugoslavia's more pressing problems.[5] In particular such a system would serve to integrate the country's economy more effectively with the world's economy by quickly indicating to the country's planners and others when mistakes in economic planning have been made. The correction of mistakes would not have to depend on occasional changes in temporarily rigid official exchange rates. Milton Friedman is surely correct when he argues that such a system "provides neither the stability of expectations that a genuinely rigid and stable exchange rate could provide in a world of unrestricted trade and willingness and ability to adjust the internal price structure to external conditions nor the continuous sensitivity of a flexible exchange rate."[6] Worse still for Yugoslavia, a temporarily rigid official exchange rate deprives the country of vitally needed information regarding its external trade position, on which a sizable part of its income depends, and a continuous mechanism for maintaining external equilibrium.

[5] See, for example, Milton Friedman, "The Case for Flexible Exchange Rates," in *Essays in Positive Economics* (Chicago: University of Chicago Press, 1953), pp. 157–203.

[6] *Ibid.*, p. 164.

15.▲

IN RETROSPECT

THE PRIVATE SECTOR

If official statements are taken at their face value, the private sector in the country will continue to play an important role in the economy. To be sure, such a role does not have the blessings of the country's more dogmatic theoreticians, who have a jaundiced view of everything outside the socialist sector. Indeed, in May 1962 some of the more zealous and influential theoreticians apparently managed to make their influence felt when the government increased the taxes imposed on private businesses sevenfold—apparently for the purpose of wiping out such activities. The pretext was the high profits obtained by such private businessmen as barbers, blacksmiths, cobblers, tailors, and pastry makers. So effective was the tax that by the end of 1962 nearly 10,000 of these craftsmen went out of business.

Unfortunately for Yugoslavia substitutes for the services of these craftsmen were not forthcoming. According to one report, Yugoslavs "found it virtually impossible in some areas to obtain the services of a plumber or electricians. To get a pair of shoes repaired in Belgrade takes a month. Belgrade's famed candy and pastry shops are nearly all closed, and the state-baked pita—a Serbian pastry filled with fruit—is no edible substitute." [1]

Conditions deteriorated so rapidly that President Tito was

[1] *Time*, March 15, 1963, p. 44.

prompted to state that "a real witch hunt was started against the alleged enrichment of artisans, and excessively high taxes were levied against them." [2] At his suggestion the matter was reviewed by the Yugoslav Parliament in March 1963, and a new tax law was passed that "would not discourage the development of crafts." Commenting on the law, the Belgrade daily *Borba* stated that "the law treats private craftsmen as an additional but significant economic branch which fits well in the system of socialist economy." [3]

It is a sad commentary on what some people of influence in the country consider as the key to national wealth that severe penalties should be placed on private economic entrepreneurship. It is sadder yet when such "wisdom" is allowed to prevail over the country's traditional espousal of free trade. The greatness and economic wealth of fourteenth-century Serbia were due in no small measure to the free trade promoted by Emperor Stefan Dušan's Law Code. This remarkable fourteenth-century document provided, among other things, for "the imposition of heavy monetary penalties on any individual regardless of rank or office who attempted to restrain either merchant or peasant from buying or selling goods, including grains, and freely bringing his wares to market." [4] Moreover, the Emperor himself was expressly subject to the law.

Centuries before many development theorists became aware that a problem existed, it would appear that Emperor Stefan Dušan had the key to the development of a country's wealth. It is little wonder that under his rule Serbia and indeed all the Balkan area reached a peak of economic development that remained unequaled for more than 500 years. In terms of economic wisdom as well as in other matters Stefan Dušan's contributions are significant.

The importance of the private sector to the country's economy is indicated imperfectly by data which suggest that in 1960 it

[2] *Ibid.*

[3] *Ibid.*

[4] Traian Stoianovich, "Conquering Balkan Orthodox Merchant," *Journal of Economic History*, June 1960, p. 236.

amounted to 22 per cent of the social product. When account is taken of the fact that the private sector has operated under adverse conditions since the war, its rate of annual economic growth of 6.5 per cent in the period 1957–60 is remarkable. Some idea of the adverse conditions under which this sector has operated is indicated by the fact that private farmers are forbidden to purchase modern machinery such as tractors except in junk yards. Official data on how well the socialist sector is doing compared to the private sector tend to disregard the obviously discriminatory conditions under which the latter sector operates. If it were afforded the same treatment as the socialist sector, the resulting data would undoubtedly tell a very different story. Such a story would not be well received by the country's more dogmatic theoreticians. If one is seeking those responsible for the wobbly performance of the country's economy in 1961–62, it would seem to rest with the intellectuals who place theoretical dogma above their country's welfare. Fortunately for Yugoslavia and its mixed type of economy, it would appear that sanity will prevail in the long run—at least to the extent of preserving a place for some modicum of private entrepreneurship.

THE SOCIALIST SECTOR

Economic activity in all of Europe slackened in the early 1960's. Bad weather and the uncertainties surrounding foreign trade are said to have been responsible. If so, it suggests that planned and relatively free economies share much the same fate when weather and foreign trade are concerned. These are elements against which a planned economy's socialist sector cannot be perfectly insulated. And, indeed, one test of a socialist sector's viability in a planned economy is how well it is able to meet foreign competition.

Though far from spectacular, the relatively better performance of Yugoslavia's economy over those of Czechoslovakia, Hungary, Poland, Rumania, and Bulgaria at this time suggests that the former's socialist sector is best able to cope with foreign trade problems. In view of the verbal and other abuse heaped on Yugoslavia by these same countries during the 1950's it must be some satisfaction to the Yugoslavs that their "approach to socialism" has at least the merit of being realistic. It would seem that these countries are becoming painfully aware that quality, variety, and efficiency are as important as impressive production statistics. Economic development is something more than merely increasing steel-production tonnages and the number of textile spindles. Bad weather and a stiffening of competition on the world market exposed the underlying weakness of low-quality and high-cost output that is characteristic of many of the countries of Eastern Europe. Fortunately for Yugoslavia and its socialist sector these characteristics are not so pronounced, though they are certainly in evidence.

The slowdown in Yugoslavia became pronounced in 1961 and continued into 1962, though by the end of the year some revival occurred. The revival was not a significant one because of the drought that plagued southeastern Europe. Even so, exports in January and February of 1962 increased 13 per cent over those of the same months in 1961, and by January and February 1963 an increase of 19 per cent had been registered over the same months in 1962. Imports, on the other hand, continued to exceed exports, and they increased by about 3 per cent in 1962 over 1961 and in 1963 by about 5 per cent over 1962.

This is in marked contrast to developments in the other socialist economies of Europe. In Rumania, for example, the drought coupled with reorganization and other socialist tinkering with the economy resulted apparently in bread rationing in such a rich province as Transylvania even though industry continued to enjoy a boom.[5] Bulgaria was so hard hit by the drought that food rationing was reinstated.[6] Poland and Czechoslovakia were little better off, with the Czechoslovak regime canceling its current five-year plan because of nonfulfillment of targets.[7] Poland ran into more trouble than at any time in the six years since the

[5] *New York Times,* April 19, 1963, p. 65. See also President Tito's remarks in *Ekonomska politika* (Belgrade), April 20, 1963, pp. 476–77.
[6] *New York Times;* April 19, 1963, p. 65.
[7] *Ibid.*

Stalinist regime ended.[8] Only Hungary apparently managed to maintain some semblance of economic progress, thanks undoubtedly to the recent "enlightenment" of the Kadar regime.[9] It is small wonder that the Yugoslav regime considers that the experiences of other socialist countries confirm its independent road to socialism. The prospects are good that Yugoslavia will continue to follow its own independent road.

YUGOSLAVIA'S UNDERDEVELOPED REGIONS

One of the most difficult problems confronting the country is the development of its relatively backward areas. The magnitude of the problem is indicated by the fact that these areas comprise about 47 per cent of the territory and about one-third of the population. They form a compact strip stretching from the country's southeast border to its northwest frontier and include the whole of the republics of Macedonia and Montenegro, the autonomous province of Kosovo-Metohija, parts of southeastern and southwestern Serbia, parts of the Dalmatian seaboard, and parts of the republic of Bosnia-Hercegovina.

The Yugoslav approach to regional development problems since the war has been to pour large sums into these southern areas from the more prosperous north through the medium of the Federal Investment Fund. But unlike the approach adopted by the Italians, who placed heavy emphasis on overhead facilities, relying on them to stimulate commodity production in southern Italy, the Yugoslavs concentrated their efforts in creating several centers of industrial development within southern Yugoslavia. According to available studies, Italy thus far has had little success even though ten years of effort and considerable resources have been devoted to the problem.[10]

To judge from available data, Yugoslav efforts, on the other hand, have been crowned with some spectacular successes. By 1957,

[8] *Ibid.*
[9] *Ibid.*
[10] See, for example, Hollis B. Chenery, "Development Policies for Southern Italy," *Quarterly Journal of Economics*, Nov. 1962, pp. 515–47.

for example, progress was so marked in the republic of Bosnia-Hercegovina that further development can now be left to the area's own resources. The republics of Macedonia and Montenegro and the province of Kosovo-Metohija have also demonstrated a vitality unknown in these areas for many centuries.

The prospects for the country's underdeveloped regions are indeed bright, though it will probably be a long time before they reach the level of the most advanced republic, Slovenia. Nevertheless, a good start has been made, and before too many years the Yugoslavs will be able to enjoy significant returns on their efforts. So successful have the Yugoslavs been in developing their southern regions that the Italians participated in a joint Yugoslav-Italian Economic Symposium in Ohrid, Macedonia, May 25–31, 1961, for the purpose of comparing notes on the economic development of their respective regions. And even the Greeks, rightly or wrongly, now view industry as the key to future development.[11]

FOREIGN TRADE

A glance at Yugoslavia's statistics on foreign trade suggests its urgent need for some kind of accommodation with the European Common Market. Otherwise the country may very well face a situation similar to that experienced in 1948, when its trade with the East broke down. In view of Britain's difficulties and Austria's fumbling attempts to achieve some sort of association with the Common Market the prospects for Yugoslavia are gloomy indeed. There is little reason to believe that its prospects are any better with the Council for Mutual Economic Assistance (Comecon), the Communist version of Western Europe's Common Market. Unfortunately for Yugoslavia it is once again in the middle.

An alternative, albeit a poor one, is the expansion of Yugoslavia's trade with its nonaligned partners. This trade, as already noted, has grown in recent years. But the type and quality of products and services required by Yugoslavia in its current state of development are not likely to be found in the world's southern tier of countries.

[11] *New York Times,* April 19, 1963, p. 60.

In view of such prospects it is easy to understand why the Yugoslavs have been arguing strenuously for free multilateral trade while at the same time espousing more favorable treatment for the world's underdeveloped countries. The possible collision of grand designs in Europe and elsewhere together with the undercurrent of mercantilism in these designs suggests that the Yugoslav course of free multilateral trade is not unrealistic—at least not for the world as a whole.

Appendix 1

EXTRACTS FROM THE STATUTES OF THE COMMUNE OF KRANJ[1]

Article 1. The commune of Kranj is a political and territorial organization administered by the workers under a system of self-government and a social and economic community which includes all the inhabitants of the district. It forms part of the district of Kranj.

Article 2. [On the composition of the commune of Kranj.] . . .

Article 3. The workers of the commune shall exercise their rights and carry out their obligations either through the people's committee of the commune, the local committees and other organs of communal self-government; or directly by taking part in the election of the representative body of the commune or the removal of its members, by attending voters' meetings and by referendum.

The communal self-government authorities exercise the rights of the commune through the organs of self-government that function in the economic organizations and social institutions or through other organs of social administration.

Article 4. In the administration of social affairs the commune shall exercise all those rights and carry out all those obligations for which the organs of self-government of the workers in the economic organizations and social institutions are not responsible, with the exception of the rights and obligations that are reserved by the Constitution or by law to the district, to the People's Republic or to the Federative People's Republic.

[1] Reprinted from *International Social Science Journal*, no. 8 (1961), pp. 442–46.

Article 5. Self-government by the workers in the commune shall be guaranteed by the Constitution. It shall be carried on in conformity with the law and in accordance with the general principles of the social order established by the socialist democracy of the People's Federative Republic of Yugoslavia.

Article 6. In matters affecting more than one commune in the district the workers of the commune shall exercise their right of self-government through representatives on the people's committee of the district or by other methods of self-government.

The rights and obligations of the organs of self-government of the district with respect to the organs of self-government of the commune shall be determined by law.

Article 7. The people's committee of the commune shall be the fundamental organ of authority of the workers.

The people's committee shall be the supreme organ of authority in the commune of Kranj and shall function within the limits of its rights and obligations.

All the organs of State administration in the commune shall be subordinate to the people's committee of the commune except where otherwise provided by law with respect to the administrative organs which are concerned with matters falling within the competence of the district, the People's Republic or the Federative People's Republic.

Article 8. The commune shall have the following rights and obligations:

It shall reconcile the individual interests of citizens with social interests in general;

It shall ensure the conditions necessary for the development of the productive forces and the continued improvement of the economic and cultural conditions of the commune;

It shall direct the economic development as a whole and apportion that part of the national revenue which is produced in the commune so as to satisfy its economic, cultural and social needs;

It shall adapt the aims and activities of the economic organizations to the general social requirements and stimulate the development of the economic organizations and the productivity of labor;

It shall administer the social property assigned for public use, in particular social property entrusted to the commune; and protect social and personal property;

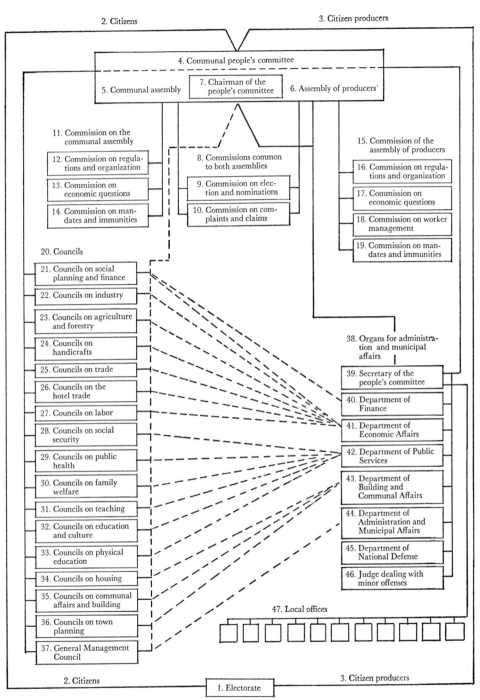

Appendix figure 1. Organization chart of the commune of Kranj.

It shall have the full right of disposal over the resources of the commune; define the obligations of the economic organizations with respect to the commune and establish the communal rates;

It shall of its own initiative organize matters of direct interest to the commune;

It shall apply the laws and all other provisions provided that the right to do so has not been expressly entrusted to other bodies, institutions or organizations;

It shall determine the structure and functions of communal institutions and organs;

It shall organize communal services, promote the development of the residential communities and help them to solve their communal and social problems;

It shall take the necessary steps to maintain and raise the level of public health;

It shall make due provision for compulsory public education and vocational training and ensure the conditions necessary for cultural development;

It shall ensure that the social security measures are duly carried out;

It shall safeguard the personal and political rights of the citizens and guarantee the legality of administrative acts;

It shall exercise supervision over the legality of the acts of autonomous institutions and organizations;

It shall protect public order and peace in the commune;

It shall discuss questions falling within the competence of the district, the People's Republic or the Federative People's Republic, or of the autonomous organization; make proposals for the solution of such questions and take part therein, in accordance with the law.

The rights of the commune of Kranj shall be exercised and its obligations shall be assumed by the people's committee of the commune itself and by its organ and institutions and by the autonomous institutions and organizations in accordance with the rules of competence laid down by the law, by this statute or by other provisions.

Article 9. The commune shall have at its disposal the resources specified by the law.

Article 10. In the exercise of its rights and obligations the commune shall act as follows through the people's committee and other organs of communal self-government:

1. It shall adopt its own economic plan and budget in complete independence.

2. It shall promulgate in complete independence such provisions as are in accordance with the powers conferred on it by law and impose administrative penalties as prescribed by law, in cases of failure to observe the said provisions.

3. It shall establish economic undertakings and communal institutions of a cultural, educational, and social character, and for the improvement of public health.

4. It shall apply directly to the laws and to the statutory provisions and shall for that purpose conduct all necessary penal and administrative proceedings, make decisions as a court of first instance and perform all administrative acts, provided that direct action in such matters is not within the competence of other organs.

5. It shall quash and declare null and void all unlawful acts performed by economic or other organizations and by institutions placed under its supervision in accordance with law.

6. It shall take all necessary steps for the management of affairs within its competence and promulgate such administrative, economic or other measures as may be requisite for that purpose.

7. It shall provide the resources necessary for the operation of the public services in the commune.

8. It shall ensure the functioning of the communal services, appoint the necessary skilled staff for that purpose, supervise their training and protect their rights.

9. It shall make recommendations to the economic organizations and self-governing institutions with respect to their activities.

10. It shall appeal to the competent authority to protect its right of self-government on every occasion when one of its rights as specified by law is prejudicially affected by any regulation or other act of a higher State organ.

Article 11. In the performance of its rights and obligations the Commune of Kranj shall not exceed the provisions of the law with respect to the citizens, economic and other organizations and social institutions.

Article 12. The commune shall exercise its rights and carry out its obligations by virtue and with the limits of the law, its own regulations and those of the superior organs of the State.

Article 13. Relations between the People's Committee of the commune and the other organs of communal self-government in all matters of common interest shall be determined by the law and by the present statute.

Article 14. Local committees shall be constituted in the territory of the commune to ensure that citizens play as large a part as possible in communal self-government and in the management of affairs that directly affect the local population.

Article 15. The People's Committee of the commune and the local committees shall for the purpose of exercising their rights derive their authority from the meetings of the voters to whose decision they shall give effect as required by law.

Article 16. The People's Committee of the commune shall make provision for the regular and lawful exercise of their judicial duties.

Article 17. The People's Committee of the commune shall assist the organs of the State in the exercise of their judicial duties.

Article 18. The commune of Kranj shall be a body corporate.

[Articles 19–126 follow.]

Appendix 2

COMMODITY LISTS ACCORDING TO FOREIGN TRADE REFORMS OF 1961[1]

I. Exports
   A. Export List of Quota Commodities:
      1. *Industrial products:* propane-butane, rolled products, electrolytic zinc, silver, bismuth, copper and copper alloy rolled and drawn products, cement, flat glass, enamelware, fittings and plumbing fixtures, sodium hydroxide, sodium carbonate, sawn soft wood, draft paper, cardboard, pasteboard, wrapping paper, writing and printing paper, all kinds of thin paper except cigarette paper, cotton and staple fibre fabrics, leather footwear, sole leather rubber footwear and egg products.
      2. *Agricultural produce:* lucerne and red clover seeds, vetch and cowpea seeds, live cattle except class I and Ia shelled eggs.
   B. Commodities Requiring Export Permits:
      1. *Industrial products:* scrap iron and iron waste, scrap machine castings, white and grey pig iron, billets, raw steel, sheets and tin-plates of all kinds and scrap, welded tubes, ferromolybdenum, calcium molybdenite, molybdenum concentrate, ferrotungsten, selenium, electrolytic copper, primary zinc, scrap and waste of non-ferrous metals and alloys, aluminum ingots, asbestos fibres, sulphuric acid, synthetic fertilizers of all kinds, blue vitrol, electrolytic sodium hydroxide, waste paper, newsprint, wool yarn, raw skins, raw hides, dressed calfskin, all kinds of flour, lard, clarified butter, butter, tal-

[1] Reprinted from *Yugoslav Survey*, June 1961, pp. 679–80.

217

low, leaf-fat, edible oil, powdered milk, blood meal, fish meal, meat and bone meal, combined concentrated livestock feed, bran sugar, dry sugar-beet shreds, oil-seed and other bast fibres, cotton yarn, synthetic yarns, "leonine" yarns, flax yarns, felt for technical and trade purposes, synthetic shoe-maker's thread, sea-weed, rabbit hair, horsehair, bolting-mills, raffia, phlox-yarn, cotton waste, raw hides and skins, natural, synthetic and reclaimed rubber, revertex and latex, linseed for industrial use, fresh sea-fish for the canning industry, cork.

2. *Consumer goods:* southern fruit (except oranges, lemons and tangerines), tea and spices, shredded coconut, stockfish, food-stuffs for children and babies, fruit juices, vegetable juices sweetened or unsweetened, unfermented, without alcohol, medicinal and other mineral waters, spirits, dessert and aro-matic wines, champagne, beer, tobacco products, tobacco ex-tracts and essences, colour film and colour photography paper, developers, fixers and chemicals for colour films and colour photography paper, artists' paints.

C. Commodities Imported on Liberalized Permits:
Waste and scrape copper and copper alloys, iron ore with over 42 per cent Fe, grey pig iron, worsted wool yarn, cocoa, tallow, palm-seed oil and linseed oil.

D. Import List of Quota Commodities:
1. *Production material and raw material:* aluminum electro-lytic and other copper, nickel, chromite, iron and steel rolled and drawn products, white pit iron, scrap iron, coke and coke dust, anthracite, pit coal, diesel oil, nitrogenous fertilizers, cement, clinker, tin and alloys, asbestos fibres, tires and inner tubes, animal feed, meal and cake with the exception of meal and cake obtained from imported linseed and poppy-seed meal and cake, logs, pitprops, coniferous fuelwood, chestnut and oak fuelwood, coniferous pulpwood, chestnut and oak tanningwood, all kinds of split logs for industrial purposes.

2. *Agricultural produce:* wheat, rye, barley, cockle, hyrid maize seed, linseed, soya bean, rape seed, sunflower seed, onion seed, foals and foal meat, live bull-calves up to six months old and their meat.

II. Imports
  A. Freely Importable Commodities:
    1. *Production material:* coking coal, graphite electrodes, aviation spirit, petroleum coke, activated carbon black, pulp, transformer oil, tungsten concentrate, manganese ore, magnesium tungsten and molybdenum wire, china clay, graphite, calcined clay, crude clay containing over 40 per cent Al_2O_3 and under 4 per cent Fe_2O_3, natural cryolite, fluorite, graphite pots, optical and unworked optical glass for further processing, raw phosphates, sulphur, tetraethyl lead, flotation reagents except xanthates, caustic soda, soda ash, tire cord, silicon carbide, sodium sulphide, rutile, additives and solvents for the petroleum industry, polymeric phosphates for detergents, dodecylbenzene for detergents, glues for the wood working industry, raw barytes bases for photographic paper, crystals for the radio and electronics industry, sulphate and sulphite cellulose, kraft paper, cotton for carding and combing, synthetic fibres and synthetic wool tops, wool, wool rags and waste, flax fibres, jute fibres, sisal fibres, manila, hogs for the canning industry, sawn soft wood, soya beans, newsprint, pharmaceutical raw materials, tanning agents.
    2. *Consumer goods:* household articles of non-metals, metals and plastics, household porcelain-ware, galvanized utensils and vessels, fancy goods, costume jewellery, chemical products for personal use, musical instruments, cameras and parts and equipment, photographic chemicals and accessories, hunting, fishing and sports equipment, bicycles and parts, bicycle tires and accessories, paper manufactures and writing and drawing paper for personal use, radio sets of all kinds including transistor radios, except parts and accessories, household electric heaters, household electric radiators, electric hot plates for households, household electric irons without controls, electric bulbs for house lighting, household electric ranges except accessories and parts, household washing machines except accessories and parts, household refrigerators except accessories and parts, television sets except accessories and parts, other electric audio-electric household appliances and accessories and parts, textile articles and leather and rubber footwear, medicines, medical instruments and sanitary

supplies, films and non-durable goods for cinema apparatus, black and white photographic paper and black and white photographic film except narrow black and white positive motion picture track and X-ray films, coffee and other food-stuffs not mentioned in the list of freely importable com-modities, salt, books, magazines and musical scores.

B. Commodities Imported on Restrictive Import Permits:

1. *Production material:* crude oil, motor petrol except aviation spirit, radio-active elements and radio-active isotopes, creo-sote oil, phosphoric fertilizers.

2. *Consumer goods:* foodstuffs except coffee and food articles mentioned in the list of freely imported commodities, sewing machines, typewriters.

3. *Capital equipment:* rail vehicles except electric and diesel locomotives, excavators and tractors, trailers of all kinds, tramways, trolley buses and trailers, refrigeration plants, textile dry-cleaning and iron equipment, cotton and wool looms and spinning-mill machinery, agricultural machinery (tractors, combines and field silage harvesters and attach-ments) , motor vehicles of all kinds including motor-cycles, cash registers.

INDEX

YUGOSLAVIA:
THE THEORY AND PRACTICE OF
DEVELOPMENT PLANNING

was composed, printed, and bound
by Kingsport Press, Inc.
for the University Press of Virginia.
The types used are Linotype Baskerville
and Bulmer for display.
The paper is Warren Olde Style
made by the S. D. Warren Company.
The book was designed by John J. Walklet, Jr.